Song Lyrics of Amurá

Other works by Amurá Oñaā

The Promise
(Poem)

Amuráti
Vol. 1
(50 Short Stories, 300 words or less)

Amuráti
(Sci-Fi & Fantasy)
Vol. 2
(50 Short Stories, 300 words or less)

The Seed
(Origin of AI)

Jonathan Hood in Close the Door Behind You

The Haven House
Co-authored with Joe Hunt

Tainted Times
(100 Days of Prose)

Of Prose and Passing Thoughts

ISBN 979-8-218-26666-0

SONG LYRICS OF AMURÁ

Songs written with the contribution of Keith Gonzales
Better Times, Better Days
Now I See You
Love Won't Let You Fall
Stroke for Stroke
Ding Dong School of the Hard Luck Blues

Song written with the contribution of Glenn Spivack
What's a Friend For?

Cover Photo by Aaron Kneile

Published by Amurá Unlimited, LLC

www.amuraunlimited.com

Dedicated to Family,
and
My Life Experience
allowing me to put
words to music.

Table of Contents

Introduction ix

Song Lyrics Early Period 1961-1970

Love as We Know It 3

Lonely 4

The One Love I Know Of 5

Who Do You Love? 6

Are You Going to Tell? 8

Lady of the Tower 10

Let's Love Again 11

I'd Give My All 12

Broken Woman 13

Sold to the Man Dressed in Red 14

Statues 16

Lord, I Want to Be With You 18

Tell Me Why 19

Suicide Family-Wise 20

Stay 21

Let's Go Home 22

Cobble-Stone Lane 24

Good Mornin' Mr. G. 26

It Really Just Begun 28

Goodbye Gentle Lady 30

Girl Outside My Window 31

The Feelin' of Love 32

Table of Contents (cont'd)

Song Lyrics Early Period 1961 -1970 (cont'd)

Where Are You Love? 34
If You Want Love 35
Goodbye 36
Love Won't Let You Fall 37

Song Lyrics From 1971 - 1980

Beggin' Again 41
Going for a Drive 42
Mind If I Stay? 43
There's Power in Love (Reggae) 44
Let's Hit the Road 46
Night School 47
Just Give Me Love 48
Love Each Other Well 50
One Night Deal 51
The Good and the Hard 52
Travelin' Lady 55
Let's Go Down to the River 56
Now You See I Love You 57
She's Like a Lonely Bird 58
Sorry Girl 59
Take Your Hold Off Me 60
Stories 61

Table of Contents (cont'd)

Song Lyrics From 1971 - 1980 (cont'd)

Take What You Need and Ride 62
Louisiana 63
Goin' Isn't Easy 64
Take Me Home, Girl 66
The Audition 68
Star 69
It's You Who I Live For 70
Love and Peace 71
Black Woman's Child 72
Waters Merge With Mine 74
Other Side of the Sea 75
How Much Longer Can We Ride? 76
Golden Day 78
Sun Overdue 79
Children, What Do They Know That We Don't? 80
What's a Friend For? 82
Everybody Wants 84
One Within One 86
If Ever I Need You (I Need You Now) . . 87
Bye, Bye, Baby 88
Considerin' (Livin' for Today) 89
Better Stay Here Till the Morning 90

Table of Contents (cont'd)

Song Lyrics From 1971 - 1980 (cont'd)

Excuses, Excuses 91
In the Streets of the City 92
Saturday Night 93
Wars in Those Days The Best Love . . . 94
The Best Love 96
Two Are Never Alone 98
Better Times, Better Days 99
Dream Lady 100
Stormy Weather 101
Be There 102
I'll Never Leave Again 103
Wine and Beer 104
If I Only Had the Time 106
Rosie 108
Sally West 109
Runaway Train 110
Crystal Mountain Morning 112
Do You Really Want Me to Leave . . . 113
The End of the Dream 114
Our Love , , , , , , , , , , , , , , , , , , 115
I Love You 116
The Performer 118
Run, Michael, Run 120

Table of Contents (cont'd)

Song Lyrics From 1971 - 1980 (cont'd)

Rock and Rollin' (Till the Break of Dawn) . 122

Song Lyrics From 1981 - 1990

Love Comes Alive 125
Love Is 126
Help Me Out 127
The Way of Things 128
I Am Self 129
What a Lovely Way to Go 130
The Hero 132
Love Says Goodbye 134
You Got Something Real 136
Just Lovin' You for a Lifetime 138
What You Gonna Do for Me? 140
I'm Prayin' for One Tonight 141
Shoot for the Sky 142
Stroke for Stroke 143
One-Way Love 144
A Kwanzaa Song 146

Song Lyrics From 1991 - 2000

Good Love, A Healing Pain 151
Crossroad 152

Table of Contents (cont'd)

Song Lyrics From 1991 - 2000 (cont'd)

When You Play with Fire 154
Another Child Is Gone 156
Ain't No Blues 158
Neath the City Lights 160
Then I See You 161
Stand Up, Stand Down 162
Lady on a Train 164
Broken Glass 166
Workin' to Be Poor 168
Genocide 170
One Can Never Tell 172
Is Anybody Out There? 174
Your Eyes 176
Drinkin' the Blues 177
Serenade 178
Heart of Gold 180
I Should've Seen It Coming 183
You Must Believe 184
Thought You Were All Alone 186
In My Darkest Hour 188
Premonition 189
Where We Comin' From? 190
Not for Sale 192

Table of Contents (cont'd)

Song Lyrics From 1991 - 2000 (cont'd)

Decisions 193
Why So Many Holes in the Road? 194
Lovin' You for Real 196
Is It True That You're Leaving? 197
Riding This White Horse 198
Black Widow 200
Come Child 202
Looking for a Place in Your Heart . . . 203

Song Lyrics From 2001 - 2010

Startin' All Over Again 207
So Glad You Came 208
So Many Lies 209
Maybe Somewhere Down the Line . . 210
Got Me Begging 212
Too Long in the Rain 213
Pain to Kill 214
Where Is the Man I Was? 216
Stay With Me 217
Take Me Home 218
Walkin' Shoes 219
Best Part of Me 220
For a Little While 221

Table of Contents (cont'd)

Song Lyrics From 2001 - 2010 (cont'd)
Silk and Lace 222
Love Sick Blues 223
Ding-Dong School of the
Hard-Luck Blues 224
Let Me See You Home 225
Living With the Truth - You're Gone . 226
Blues of a Soldier 228
Rain Man 230
Come on In 231
Is It True What They Say About You? . 232

Song Lyrics From 2011 - 2020
What Could Have Been Your Life . . 235
Was This Meeting by Design? 236
It Ain't Over 238
Mary in the Garden 240
Take My Burden Down 242

Epilogue 243

Introduction

I started playing guitar around 1964 – 65. It was an old Stella guitar my father had purchased in the 50s from a pawn shop on 145 Street between Broadway and Amsterdam avenues. I remember him taking me up there with him. He might've been interested in learning to play music as he loved to listen to his jazz records. However, he never found the time, and the guitar found a nesting place under the basement stairs of our house in the Bronx once we joined the exodus out of Harlem, New York.

With the influence of the Beatles, Dylan, and other musicians/songwriters, I became interested in the instrument. Starting with broomsticks and three other nerdy friends, I began a journey I never thought I would take. One that I would love for the rest of my life. I dug up my father's dusty guitar and, against my father's wishes, started teaching myself how to play.

"Why this book?" It's not like I'm some well-known celebrity. Someone that society, at this point in time, made a poignant decision to knight me with a thorny crown representing some level of fame. Maybe Ego is up to no good and is making a last-ditch effort to lay claim to past achievements it can call its own, so it can drink from the fountain of pride and remark, "See, you did do something! You were more than just a bag of wind blowing out hot gaseous vapors."

My parents named me Christopher Newton (which is probably already more than I wish to divulge). My mother was raised a Catholic, and she named all her children after the patron saints. Now, I don't want to churn this into some autobiography. Really, I can't see any reason for skating in that rink.

I think I'd just like putting some of my shit in an organized pile, so folks won't step in it along their journey through life. At the very least, it should allow them to walk around it if they choose or plow on through. I had an early interest in poetry. Being a lonely and introverted soul, words on paper came naturally to me. And so I just fashioned them to the strumming of a guitar.

As in my case, sometimes a person may assume that they haven't done much or consider their efforts as a big waste of time. It was a product of years of flights of depression. I feel that depression can be the fuel for an artist in any medium, as it was for me. It was a painful journey where music would pull me toward the light long enough to stop my trip down the rabbit hole.

Ever notice how much we reveal about ourselves when talking in a comfortable space? As lovely as it is, I don't want to talk too much. After writing hundreds of songs, I realize they may reveal more about myself than I ever intended. There's no sense in repeating myself.

I'm pretty much like everyone else, occupying a vessel in this realm of life. And applying what I understand by coloring the circumstances around my essence. Something I've done before and will invariably do again as far as I am concerned.

I know my song lyrics will capture a lot about myself. Being raised a Baptist Christian, the influence is there, even now when I consider myself more of a spiritualist. There's no sense denying any part of my life that molded me into the person I am today. It's been 360 degrees since birth.

I collected the song lyrics and placed them in groups of decades. They are necessarily in sequence. I hope the reader will witness my poetic growth as I worked to develop my writing style in the later years.

I must admit, I did surprise myself at the number of songs written. I knew I needed to contain them between the covers of a book. There are so many half-written, unfinished pieces of work that I couldn't include. There are also songs I'm unable to find, tapes misplaced and son on. I stopped writing songs after a pair of strokes in 2010, turning more toward writing stories and prose. Finding it difficult to play my guitar and recover my style, I wrote only a few lyrics in the last decade. I turned my expressional outlet to writing short stories and fictional works. I hope you find a few gems in the body of work. Thank you.

Song Lyrics

Early Period
1961 to 1970

Love as We Know It

Love as we know it
    Is just a game,
And we live by the rules
    That we follow each day,
Soon our hearts will discover
    What we already knew,
That Love is just a game.

Dreams as they come
    Must one day fade,
Like the love we have shared
    All these long lovely days.
And we'll find at the moment
    Of when we're making love
That Love is just a game.

Love as we know it
    Is just a game,
And we live by the rules
    That we follow each day,
Soon our hearts will discover
    What we already knew,
That Love is just a game.
    That Love is just a game.

Lonely

I never thought that I could be so lonely, lonely.
I never thought a time would come
When loving you was to love someone
Whose heart is bare,
There's no one there, when I call.

I never thought my dreams could be so empty, empty.
I never thought our love could die,
You turned and said,
"My darling, I must go
Before you plead for more of my love."

Bridge:
Alone to myself
Thoughts of you burning,
Thoughts of you turning
My world upside down.
There's no one around
To comfort me.

I never thought that I could be so lonely, lonely.
I never thought a time would come
When loving you was to love someone
Whose heart is bare,
There's no one there, when I call,
When I call.

The One Love I Know Of

Behind all the people and folk
There's one love I know of.
Behind all the fire and smoke
There's one love I know of.
Strange things are happening to me.
I love you, can't you see?

In one heart I felt full of stone,
There's one love I know of.
And when I'm sad and alone,
There's one's love I know of.
My heart has turned away from me.
I love you, can't you see?

Bridge:
That's why I love the way you walk,
Love the way you walk.
Cherish everything you do and say.
That's why I want to hold your hand,
Make you understand
What I really need to say.

In one small and gorgeous girl,
There's one love I know of.
Please share that love with one,
The one love I know of,
We will be happy eternally
We'll love each other for eternity.

*First love song in my young teens.

Who Do You Love?

The last time I had a talk with you,
We were tight, oh so right,
It was a dream come true.
But now you're causing me pain.
You tell me that your life has change.
I wanna know -

Chorus:
Who do you love, do you love, do you love?
Who do you love, do you love?

I just don't seem to understand,
From yesterday to today,
You're in love with another man.
You say you love me too,
And it's so hard for you to choose.
Ah, come on (chorus repeat)

Bridge:
Oh, I'm tryin' to be cool,
So just make up your mind,
I'm just about to lose my head.
Please tell me that you're foolin' this time
And I'll forget every word I said,
Just tell me (chorus, break)

And now you're causing me pain
You tell me that your mind has changed.
I wanna know (chorus)

It's all right, I've been through this before,
The names have changed, it's all arranged
    For me to walk on out that door.
But you ain't gettin' off light,
Before I leave this house tonight
I'm gonna know (chorus, repeat to end)

Are You Goin' to Tell?

I fell into a hole
    And in it was hiding War.
He said to me, "Don't tell,
    I don't want to be used anymore.
I'm hiding from the dead,
    The streams of blood that I have left.
Go tell your leaders now,
    I'm not for Peace, I'm just for Death."

"Have you seen the fear I have
    In the faces of men who've met their fate.
Have you seen their loved-ones too,
    Who stay at home in patient wait.
Don't come here to search for Peace.
    He's dying from a fight we had.
Your President does pay well,
    But I didn't kill Peace, so I know he's mad."

Bridge:
"Remember this," he said
    "Peace is not that bad, if you can get it by yourselves.
Don't ask a third party like me to help you out.
    Why do you think I can help you?
Go find your Peace and try to make him live.
    You're killin' him with each war you ask me to give.
Go find him yourselves, go find your God,
    Asking me to kill won't solve your problems."

"Your time is drawing nigh,
 I hear the footsteps of another man.
He's come to make a deal
 For me to destroy another land.
His eyes seem slanted now
 Or is that a flag with stars and stripes?
If he finds I'm hiding here,
 I'll have to destroy everybody's life.

If he asks, are you goin' to tell?
If he asks, are you goin' to tell?
If he asks, are you goin' to tell?

Lady of the Tower

I follow the path of my lady dear,
Toward a forest near sways her steps.
And from the woods I hear her laughter clear,
I let fall a tear and briefly rest.

I sigh as I enter this sea of trees,
For in the midst of these I come to feel
The presence of my lady near,
For her song I hear, though she stays concealed.

Bridge 1:
She left in such silence it woke me,
A tempest within had begun,
And with her the love we existed on
Simply went along
And shattered the sun.

Her voice still lingers within the air,
She doesn't care, time has shown.
And yet my soul still yearns for her
As it tries to stir the love we've known.

I reach a clearing as time goes pass,
In a field of grass - a tower high.
A tower made from her heart of stone,
And its zenith shown, it touched the sky.

Bridge II:
She cried from atop, "Go away lover!
Loving you was all wrong.
Too high am I to touch you ground
Find another sound,
Then sing your song.

Let's Love Again

Place your hand in mine,
Put your fears away,
Trust me one last time,
I need you today.
Given all we have,
With the hurt and the pain -
Some might say we won't make it girl,
But let's love again.

Let me touch your heart,
And show you how I feel.
Sometime being apart,
Helps to make love real.
Real enough to know
When tears fall like rain.
I should've never said goodbye,
Let's love again.

Chorus:
Let's love again.
I never knew how much I needed you.
Let's love again, and again, and again,
Let's love again.

Talk:
Sometimes we don't see the beauty that lies within. The love, the patience, the understanding that someone like you gives. And while I was out there chasing every dream under the sun, I realized that no matter what dreams I fulfilled. It wouldn't be complete without you.
And so, I'm asking you now. My heart in my hand, let's share this dream called life. Let's love again.

(Repeat 1st verse and fade with chorus repeating.)

I'd Give My All

For fleeting moments lost in timeless years,
I'd give my all, give my all.
For enchanted words which no one else can hear,
I'd give my all, give my all..
For the lovely sound of spring.
For the love only you can bring to me,
I'd give my all to you and to our love,
And to our love.

For soft sweet lips that hold a tender kiss,
I'd give my all, give my all.
For gentle hands that hold me and caress
I'd give my all, give my all.
For the meaning of night and day,
For the cherished words you say to me,
I'd give my all to you and to our love.
And to our love.

For distant dreams which only come at dawn,
I'd give my all, give my all.
For those precious scenes when you show your charm,
I'd give my all, give my all.
For the romance that may be mine
As our love begins to shine brighter.
I give my all to you and to our love,
And to our love. (Repeat last line.)

Broken Woman

Broken woman, broken woman,
Tell me now, I need to know.
Is your heart prepared to love again?
If not let me go.

Broken woman, broken woman,
Must your broken heart brake mine?
Is our love a star within the dark?
If so, let it shine.

Bridge:
I know it's hard to find a way.
Tell me how, I need to know.
Is your heart prepared to love again.
If not, let me go.
If not, let me go.

(Repeat 1st verse and fade.)

Sold to the Man Dressed in Red*

There is a man who's selling his wares
As the people are crowded below.
His wares sell for cheap
As he taps out a beat,
As his buyers are beginning to show.

"First item up for sale
A crossed with some blood stained nails.
This robe is thrown in free,
Sorry, but there's no key.
Man has lost the trail
To the place the bearer be.

Chorus I:
Ah! Have we a bid or have we a price?
Don't worry, it's owner is dead.
Ah! There's a hand, for a penny
And it's sold to the man dressed in red.

Why wait for the bomb to come?
Here's a bomb and some guns.
Go on home and start a war,
Then come on back, buy some more.
On the way back, close the door
And tell me who won.

Chorus II:
Ah! Have we a bid or have we a price?
It's for Peace remember, they said.
Ah! There's a hand, for a penny
And it's sold to the man dressed in red

Here a pile of good dreams lie,
For these dreams men have died.
Nightmares, have become of these
Just to fill our leaders' needs.
Get on the ground, down on your knees
And dream over again.

Chorus III:
Ah! Have we a bid or have we a price?
It's to dream when you're in your bed.
Ah! There's a hand, for a penny
And it's sold to the man dressed in red.

Last item, now's your chance,
Come on closer take a glance -
A nice strong soul, that's still young
And there's more where this came from.
Come up here and pick you one,
I'm selling them cheap.

Chorus IV:
Ah! Have we a bid or have we a price?
More souls to help you when you're dead.
Ah! There's a hand, for a penny
And it's sold to the man dressed in red.
Sold to the man dressed in,
Sold to the man dressed in red."

*A song my father, who didn't support in my interest in music, "If you can't make money from it, leave it alone," he would say about any of the arts. Well, he actually enjoyed it, asking me to play it in church one Sunday.

Statues

Woke up one morning to find myself lost in
A world in which people were gone.
Statues about me of friends that I once knew
All caught in the act of their deeds.

Statues of men are before me,
Caught in the act of their deeds.
Some sinning right before me
And my eyes
Slip across the room
Lost in silent gloom
As I gaze at my friends all around.

Going downstairs in my building
I noticed two statues below,
One held a gun and a bullet was hung,
Just suspended there.
Captured by the air
While another was piercing the stone.

Out on the street I came running,
As a blind man was counting his change,
Caught in the act
With his cane still intact
As his eyes could see,
As he grinned with glee
Cause he fooled all the others around.

Down two block just before me
A fire was ravaging high.
A woman had thrown
All her wealth and her stones
Just to save them first
Now she'll need a hearse
And her stones and her wealth will be pawned.

Standing on corners like pillars,
Policemen were guarding the town,
Except for that cop
By the shady bus stop,
Who had snuck a drink
Who would dare to think
That this wino was guarding your life.

FLASH!!! I read on the paper.
Two countries were fighting a war.
I looked in the sky
And beheld with a cry,
A huge missile there,
Not suspended there,
But was coming at me at full speed.

Then I woke up.

Lord, I Want to Be With You

Lord, I want to be with you.
All the day,
Closer I pray.
All the time,
All of my life
In each and every way.

Lord, you got to be with me,
All the time,
Blessings divine.
Closer to you.
As that is true.
I give you all that's mine.

Lord, I want to be with you.
In times of strife,
Beyond this life.
Eternally,
Let me be free.
From now till the end of time.

Tell Me Why

Chorus:
Just give me one good reason I can understand,
Some true words as you hold my hand.
Tell me why, why, why,
You don't want to stay.

I'm not the last to know
I saw it long ago.
I tried to hide the pain,
But it's too much to bare.
Caring when no one cares.
Our love is not the same. (Chorus)

If what you feel inside
Is so bad you can't rely
On our love to find a way.
Don't let it get you down.
I'll always be around,
Here by your side I'll stay. (Chorus)

Bridge:
Let me, let me help you.
Let me share all your joy and pain.
Tell me, cause it matter much to me.
I don't want your love in vain.

(Repeat 2nd verse and chorus, repeating 1st line of chorus.)

Suicide Family-Wise*

The street is bare
    A breeze floats by,
It chills the air
    And it moves the sky.
And on this street a figure's walkin',
    A silhouette of a man.
The wind whirls out a sound of warning,
    A gun enclosed in his hand.

Four blocks behind,
    A dim lit room.
A house of pine,
    Yet filled with gloom.
For in this house three bodies lying,
    Their faces lost in fear.
Their streams of life are now just flowing;
    The reddest merge of a love so dear.

His footsteps stop,
    His hand to his head;
A bullet is dropped,
    His body falls dead,
And on this street a body lying,
    His problems washed away.
They flow with his blood
    And it flows toward his love.
Tomorrow is someone else's day.

*Played song in college classroom, teacher asked, seeing me with guitar. After song, she asked me to sing it again after class and promptly scheduled me to see a psych counselor. I suppose it was a matter of "better safe than sorry."

Stay

My city life is changing
I need some rearrangin'.
It's getting hard to survive.
These bills I cannot pay up.
I find I got to make up lies.
It's breaking my heart.

Chorus:
Stay, oh my baby, don't go away.
I need your strength to strengthen my own.
Stay, oh my baby, don't go away.
I need your strength to strengthen my own.

This daily grind is wearing.
I got no taste for bearing
This heavy load anymore.
And what's the use of trying,
When I see my world dying, girl.
It's you I live for.

(Chorus)

My woman says she's leaving,
I just can't take this beating.
My life is being torn apart.
I'm under so much pressure,
And now my only treasure goes.
It's breaking my heart.

(Chorus to end.)

Let's Go Home

Let's go home, someone is waiting.
Aren't you tire of the ride?
Good God, it's been so long,
And oh, my hear is aching
For the love that's on the other side.
Let's go home, to years of love and warmth,
The springtime of our life,
And oh, all the friends we laughed and cried with.
Memories so hard to hide.

Let's take time to remember faces
Of those we touched along the way.
The joy and pain we felt in places,
The echoes of our yesterdays.
How we cried when shadows fill our lives,
When burning bridges barred the way.
But in time, toward home we start to wander,
Closer to love, day by day.

> Chorus:
> Oh, let's go home
> And express the love we feel inside.
> Remembering to wear a smile.
> For when we share love
> We make a home to live in all the while,
> Live in all the while.

Let's go home, not to end the journey,
But to rest from this speed at which we ride.
Miles per hour and a world still turning.
There's no safe speed, if we're all to die.

Chorus:
Just head for home,
,And express the love you feel inside,
Remembering to wear a smile,
For when we share love,
We make a home to live in, all the while.
To live in all the while,
To live in all the while,
To live in all the while.

Cobble-Stone Lane

The scenery's lost in the deep shade
Of the clouds which pass overhead.
The governess adheres to the growth rate
As the major reclines in her bed.
And outside the major's wife is searching
Losing poise and going insane.
For her earlier life was a smooth road
And now she's on Cobble-Stone Lane

Now riding hard is the major
Making time on a bartender's maid.
The swears and jest 'neath a cool smile,
The deep imprint of where they just laid.
The tavern is filled with young suckers
And upstairs a man with no name
Is popping the springs 'neath a young maid,
And introducing her to Cobble-Stone Lane

Now somewhere in town there's a rumor
Of a man whose waking the dead.
By going against the Good Book
And writing it over while he's in bed
The town folk are completely baffled
At the number of maids he has claimed.
They want his head 'neath the guillotine blade
Down the street from Cobble-Stone Lane

Bridge:
One day the major was riding the wrong road.
He broke her limit and was going too fast.

Then came a scream 'neath the soft sheets
As the major was giving his last.
The scream had cause a disturbance
And with footsteps there came a loud crash.
For his wife just happened to be passing by
Out of touch and completely deranged.
She burst in and found him exhausted
And threw him out onto Cobble-Stone Lane.

With arm about his neck and gun to his head
They marched in silent parade.
His covering was bare and he froze as he stared
At he vision that would end his charade.
His head was thrust 'neath the large blade
And with her head, she had done the same.
She shot at the rope which held the huge blade
And now blood flows down Cobble-Stone Lane.

Now a moral can never explain babe,
Why men have Cobble-Stone Lanes.
Yet some men will find it amusing,
While other just can't complain.
For the highways are smooth up until the tollbooths
And not paying can cause a great change.
And at the speed we're travelin' we'll get busted
As we go chargin' down,
chargin' down,
chargin' down Cobble-Stone Lane.

Good Morning Mr. G.*

Good morning Mr. G.
What's it gonna be today?
Won't you hang your hat and coat
On the hook on the wall.
You got time for a cup of tea
And you've got time to see nations fall.
Read the headlines and hear the call
Of the watchman who turns away.
Your wallet's filled with photographs
Of a time that was, if you recall,
When simple peace was dreamt by all,
But now nations have gone astray.

Good morning Mr. G.
How's your life coming along these days?
Guess I shouldn't mention wars
Or topics outside your range.
Shall we talk about your early life,
When things and places had a name,
When what you did was all in vain
For it made you what you are today?
Between you and others, there's a no-man's land
And there no peace, for peace brings you shame;
For you run screaming, "I'm not to blame!
It's those others across the way."

Bridge:
Your daydream world
Has long since been decayed,
You're trying to touch other lives,
When yours has been untouched fore days.

Yes, you can stay a while, Mr. G.,
    But kindly cast your pearls the other way,
For the swine are grunting too loud to hear
    What the auctioneer is trying to sell.
So drink your tea and think a while
    For the next bells you hear may be the chimes of hell.
So when you go around thinking that you're really swell.
    Well baby, the mirror's the other way.
So look on past your image, before it fades
    To see your vicious friends lying where you one fell,
But they own the last laugh, cause you know damn well
    That you house is crumbling
        And your foundation is in decay.

*Mr. G was meant for Mr. Government.

It's Really Just Begun

Your chance is here,
There's no one near,
You can be yourself.
The cage is bare,
There's no one there,
Uncover yourself.
Caste all your worlds aside,
Take of the veil that covers your eyes,

With open eyes you can see far,
With open mind you can be far.

Crystallize and change your time,
Sparkle bright and change my mind.

Like a bird you soar up in the sky,
Passing all that might be and saying bye,
Bye because it's over,
When it really just begun.

Have I asked too much
To try to touch
Your other side?
To speak to you,
To cherish too
What reflections hide.
Just bring your path close to mine,
Let the clouds break and let the sun shine.

With open heart you can feel far,
With open soul you'll go free far.

Touch my hand and lose your doubt,
Love within and love throughout.

Like a bird I'll soar up in the sky,
Lift your wings and settle to my side.
Because I need you
And up above
We'll chance on love
And down to earth we'll come.
So when visions fade
Don't say good day
Cause it's really just begun.

Goodbye, Gentle Lady

Goodbye, gentle lady.
Somehow I pictured you
    As my long lost star in the sky;
I idolized you so.
I didn't know
    That somehow stars would make me cry.

Yeah, take it easy.
Don't you worry now,
    Just don't say you can feel my pain.
It's not the same.
Go on, won't you please,
    No sense staying, my eyes filled with rain.

    Chorus:
    Just (So) don't close that stairway door.
    Leave it open to the sky.
    For should the stars come out once more,
    I want to see you, see you passing by me.

Goodbye, gentle lady,
Sure, we had good times,
    We could take each other high,
So starry eyed were we,
Tenderly.
    Yet somehow love just passed us by.

(Chorus and 1st verse, repeating: That somehow stars could make me cry.)

Girl Outside My Window

There's a girl outside my window.
She looks as nice as can be.
There's a girl outside my doorstep.
I hope this girl, she loves me.

Chorus I:
Cause I love this girl, and I alway will.
As I gaze upon my window sill.
I hope this girl, she loves me.
She love me.

There's a girl that I dream of,
To me she is so fine.
There's a girl within my heart,
I hope to make this girl mine.

Chorus II:
Cause I need this girl, and I need her now,
Always will and I guess somehow,
I hope this girl, she loves me.
She loves me.

The Feeling of Love

Chorus:
Love, the feeling of love.
The feeling of love surrounds you,
Oh love, the feeling of love.

Going downstairs
On a soft cloud of air,
As your friends just stand by,
They all watch you.
Lost in a dream
With your mind in between
The twilight of two worlds
Which surround you.
Lost in a daze,
With your mind, now you pray
As you gaze at the way
She is looking.
And with your eyes
Opened wide to the sky
As you sigh, asking why
She's so loving?

(Chorus)

Walking around
With your head pointed down
As you ponder life's future
Before you.
Knowing that life
Will be long with the one

Who cherishes
    And adores you.
Risking a glance
    Now you ask for a chance
To share love and romance
    With her always.
Down in your heart
    Feelin' so far apart.
And you pray for a start
    In your own way.

    (Chorus)

For every man,
    There's a ring in his hand.
Just waiting for the right girl
    To wear it.
Searching the stars
    And wandering far,
For a love that is home
    Where he left it.
How many times
    Must a person draw nigh
To decide and to find
    That there's love.
A feeling so pure,
    And your soul know for sure.
For you sorrows to cure,
    There is love.

    (Chorus to end)

Where Are You Love?

"I'll be here, waiting anxiously."
Those were the words my woman said to me.
And how I, I wanted to believe,
But, where are you, where you love?

I had to leave, had to go away.
And with a kiss, you said you would remain,
And keep love brighter than a flame,
But, where are you, where are you love?

Bridge:
Oh, it's so hard to believe
You're gone with my heart.
Vanished from my sight,
Off into the night.

Chorus:
Where are you love?
Where are you love?
Where are you love?
Where are you, where are you love?

There's more to this than a simple lie.
There's must be more, if it keeps you from my side.
I saw the love, I saw it in your eyes.
So where are, where you love?

If by some chance, you feel it in your heart,
Feel the pain that's tearing me apart.
Reach out, reach out and tell me -- where are you?
Oh, where are you, where are you love?

(Repeat bridge and chorus to end.)

If You Want Love

Who will read the silent memoirs
 Of a lover who has passed away?
Dreams were his to dream, but he dreamt
 His life away.
Waiting for the perfect love he sat
 And hoped she would pass his way.
She never came, ah nah, she never came.

Lovely lady, love is coming,
 Why must you face the other way?
Are your eyes too blind to see
 Love comes in different ways.
You change your posture, change your lifestyle
 Hoping others will turn your way,
Be yourself, baby, come on and be yourself, baby
 And Love will come today.

Bridge:
Love is running wild and free
And spreading rays of light,
While we sit chained to memories
And in the darkness fight.
 In the darkness fight.

Looking lonely through some window,
 Hoping Love will fall from the sky.
These aren't the ways to find what you really
 Need inside.
Feelin' shame and guessing games
 Won't bring the Love you've been trying to find,
If you want Love, you must make Love
 Then all the world is thine.

Goodbye

Comes a time when you just got to leave,
You memorized the words that will set you free.
Stage light -- cue cards -- you do your routine,
    Rehearsing everyday.

You tell your friends what's on you mind.
How your romance is just a waste of time.
Convince -- yourself -- until you're resigned
    With what you're gonna say.

    Chorus:
    But no matter how many words are spoken,
        They only hear
    Goodbye, goodbye, goodbye.
    A word that makes us cry.
    Goodbye, goodbye, goodbye.
    The tears are in their eyes.

Comes the day that you feel is right.
Nervousness makes you wait for the night.
Act IV -- scene III -- you're feelin' the fright,
But you got to end the play.

    (Chorus, repeat and fade.)

Love Won't Let You Fall
(Written with Keith Gonzales)

(First voice)
Where is the lover,

(Second voice)
The one who told you

That he would be true

Forever.

Kept your head filled with dreams

Eyes filled with tears,
ain't it true?

So why are you so all alone?

Do you feel like a fallen
stone?

Chorus:
From the top of mountain,

You can see all.

Just reach out forever,

Love won't let you fall.

Feeling uneasy,

All that surrounds you

Seems so confused.

So shaky.

Feelings inside too heavy to hold,

Burning through

Don't frown, try givin' all the love

That you need.

Touch, feel, aim for the sky

Aim free.

(Chorus to end)

Song Lyrics From 1971 to 1980

Beggin' Again

I met a man who was in need of a dime.
He said, "I know that to beg is a crime,
But I sure need that bottle of wine.
So, here I am, beggin' again."

I gave him a dime and said, "What's the score?"
He said, "You know how it is when you can't take anymore.
A simple case of the camel's last straw.
So, here I am, beggin' again."

Chorus:
"I was high society
Then my world came my world came down on me.
I was upper-middle class.
Now my friends, they call me an
Ass-sk me no questions, I'll tell you no lies;
You can't build castles with dreams in the sky.
Well, I still dream, so I beg to get by,
And here I am, beggin' again."

(Break and chorus)

"Don't trouble yourself," is what he said,
"The most time people fall is when they're ahead.
And who's to care if I'm alive of dead?
So, here I am, beggin again."

"Words of wisdom you won't hear from me.
So, get on out of here, boy, and just let me be.
It's my time to get dimes for free,
And here I am, beggin' again."

(Chorus - repeat and fade with last line.)

Goin' for a Drive

Goin' for a drive in the morning sun.
Got get away from this busy city
For a little while.
Gonna get in my car and go.

Gonna find a breeze with a hilltop sunrise.
Neath a shady tree gonna find a dream,
And take it home with me.
Gonna take in the day real slow.

Bridge:
I'm in need of an open space where I can breathe.
Gonna make my own paradise where I'll be free.

(Repeat 1st verse)

Goin' for a drive. (Repeat and fade.)

Mind If I Stay

Mind if I stay awhile.
We'll spend the night together
With dreams for two.
We'll share both joy and love
The evening through.
Let me spend this night with you.

Mind if I hold your hand.
Let me kiss your lips
Just one more time.
Let your heart and soul
This night be mine.
To last forever my love.

Bridge:
Every night I dream of you
To the stars in the sky I whisper your name.
Heaven and earth couldn't exist without you.
And if you left me, I would never be the same.

So don't mind if I ask you girl
Or when I hold you close to me.
For in our memory this will always be
The night you gave you love to me.

There's Power in Love (Reggae)

I've seen many suffer,
    Cause they're holdin' back on love.
Won't talk to a brother,
    Cause the brother ain't good enough.
I count all the faces
    On a downtown subway ride.
I see all anger.
    What the people tryin' to hide?

Chorus:
There's power in love.
Don't keep your love in an ivory tower.
There's power in love.
You've got to use it, cause in love there's power.

People raisin' children
    With never a word to say.
No words to encourage,
    No words to show the way.
Children killin' children
    Like playing some childhood game.
Grown-ups shake their heads,
    Cause the don't know who to blame.

Chorus:

Bridge:
Love, love, love, there's power in love (repeat 8x)

Oh, so many people
    Put their love away.
Save it for the New Year,
    Or some wet and rainy day.
Years go on by them,
    Like water down the drain.
"And there's no love in the world,"
    They say over and over again.

(Chorus and bridge to end.)

Let's Hit the Road

Put on some clothes and grab a hat.
Get it all together in one second flat.
Goin' for a ride in a very mean
    Blue-chrome, thunder-buster, funky machine.

Finally got the word,
It's time to hit the road.
Foot to the floor, we're gonna
    Play some rock and roll.

We'll take the road like a piece of cake,
80 to 100, the hell with the brakes.
Can't stop now, don't break the stride.
    Feel the rhythm, ride, mama, ride.

Finally got the word,
It's time to hit the road.
Foot to the floor, we're gonna
    Play some rock and roll.

Chorus:
Let's hit the road, hit the road (repeat 8x)

(Repeat 1st verse and chorus to end.)

Night School

Savin' your money,
Yeah, keep savin' it, honey.
Don't spend a cent, nah.
Keep savin' it up so you can go to night school.

Chorus;
Who wants it
Can get it at night school.
Who wants it
Can get it at night school.

There's no speculation,
You'll get your education.
It may get physical,
The technical things, we'll leave behind, it's me and you.

(Chorus)

Bridge:
General instruction's my major function
And this just may take all, all night long.
If you're advance, then let's take a chance
Let's go for the diploma or anything you want.

(Chorus)

I know I can reach ya,
Just let me be your teacher.
We'll go for high score,
The feelin' you get when you pass the test is ooh, ooh, oooh.

(Chorus to end.)

Just Give Me Love

Baby, you give me lots of treasures,
Give my body pleasures --
    Yeah, you do it nice.

You got a voice as sweet as honey,
My days are bright and sunny,
    Since you touched my life.

Darlin', the way you move your body,
You give me quite a lot babe
    Without thinkin' twice.

Bridge:
You give me so, so much
I wonder can you really see.
With all you're givin' me
There's just one thing I need --

Chorus:
Just give me love,
That sweet, sweet love,
That down home love,
Just give me love, love, love.

Ah, baby, let's not make a scene now,
You know exactly what I mean now.
    So be honest with yourself.

You know I give from where my heart is,
Not only from my pocket.
    You keep your love on a shelf.

(Bridge/chorus)

Baby, you give me lots of treasures,
Give my body pleasures --
Yeah, you do it nice.

Darlin', understand what I'm sayin'.
It's not that I'm complainin'.
It's so we can love each other right.

(So -- repeat chorus to end of song.)

Love Each Other Well*

Take my hand, touch my heart,
Share my dreams, hold me close, never part.
Be the love in my life.
These things do, in the hope that we might . . .

Chorus:
Learn to love each other well,
Love each other well,
Love each other, love each other well.

Care for me when I'm down, sing your song,
Lift me up and surround me.
Just be there, when I call,
These things do, so we can all . . . (chorus)

Bridge:
I want to share
All I have,
All I have with you.

I'll take your hand, touch your heart,
Share your dreams, hold you close, never part.
I'll be the love in your life.
These things I'll do, in the hope that we might . . .

(Chorus - repeat and fade.)

*While in college, a friend, who was a singer, asked me to write his girlfriend a song for her birthday. Long story short, his girlfriend was later to become my wife.

One Night Deal

Evening has hit the town,
And I'm yearning, really burnin'.
There she is, givin' me the eye,
Yeah, she's cookin', so good lookin'.

Chorus:
Oh, it's a one night deal.
Oh, baby, baby, it's a one night deal.
So let's make it real,
You say you're love's for free.
This I gotta see.

It's alright, we can spend the night
Over my place, into your space.
If you don't mind, we can kill some time
By gettin' close, so much closer. (Chorus)

Bridge:
You say you need good lovin'
If only for a while.
So I'll just keep on comin'
Until I cramp your style.
Then you can pick up your things and go,
Cause (chorus)

(Repeat 1st verse and chorus to end.)

The Good and the Hard

She lived her life -- a fairy tale,
She always thought that good prevailed.
Well, maybe it used to,
But she swears, "It still do!"

And at the age of seventeen,
With daddy's bucks and limousines,
She'd use you,
Oh who she'd use you.

Chorus I:
And every night she gave a show
To men and boys alike, you know.
They cried when she would go,
But she had to prove that good prevailed.
All the men in the county jail say,
"She's so good, we know,
She's so good, she's so good, we know."

He fought his way through nursery rhymes.
He lived a life on borrowed time.
No dreaming,
Only scheming.

And at the age of twenty-one,
Life was hard, and just for fun,
He'd use you
Oh, how he used you.

Chorus II:
And every night he gave a show
To women and girls alike, you know.
They cried when he would go,
But he had to prove how hard he was.
The women agreed, because they say,
"He's so hard, we know,
He's so hard, he's so hard, we know."

Bridge I:
They were to meet one fine day,
Their stars were crossed and they were on their way.
And fate would chance to let love start
For the good and the hard,
The good and the hard.

And so it was, it came to pass,
They swore that it was love at last.
No foolin',
They were droolin'.

She was so good, it blew his mind.
He was so hard, she'd come on time.
The craving
Had them raving.

Chorus III:
And every night they were the show,
It was so good and hard you know.
They cried when each one would go.
But then one night her dad found out.
He cut the funds and threw her out, saying,
"You're to good, you know.
He's so hard and you're too good, you know."

The Good and the Hard (Cont'd)

Bridge II:
Well the days grew hard and the times got tough
They'd curse it out, then he got rough.
And then one night, he dropped his guard,
Goodbye to the good and the hard.
The good and the hard

She lived her life - a fairy tale
And mumbles in some county jail.
"I don't mind
Doing time."

He lays beneath the earth somewhere.
A cometary - no one was there.
No dreamin'
No meanin'.

That's how it was with the good and the hard,
The good and the hard.

Travelin' Lady

Take you time, travelin' lady friend.
Take the weight from off your shoulders
And let your troubles end.

Chorus:
Travelin' lady smile,
Travelin' lady stay a while.

Lend a hand, touch a heart today.
Let the light within another's eyes
Help to show the way.
Come on, come on, come on, come on,
Come on, come on, come on, come on, (chorus)

Take your time, time, time, time,
time, time, time, time,
And find out who you are.
If you don't, no sense in runnin', baby.
Ah, nah, nah, nah, ...(chorus)

Bridge:
Don't you know that
Life is what you make it.
Can't fake it, (you know you can't fake it)

(Repeat verses 1 and 2 and end.)

Let's Go Down to the River

Let's go down, down to the river.
Let us stay there for awhile.
Let us sing the songs that bring men together,
As we walk this quarter mile.

Let's read the signs and raise up the banners
As we march long side the shore.
And children, children, children who cannot
See the meaning,
Guess you'll never know the score.

Chorus;
Let's go down, down to the river,
Let's go down, down to the river,
Let's go down, down to the river, now (Repeat)

Bridge:
If you cleanse your life,
You will surely, surely find
A simple peace of mind.

Let's go down, down to the river
Where the peaceful waters flow,
Where the sun shines high over Eden
And the winds of freedom blow.

Take a hand, gather together
Give a friend the gift of love,
The joy of Heaven is within you
Let your star shine high above.

(Chorus: repeat, bridge, and chorus to end.)

Now You See I Love You
(with Keith Gonzales)

I use to know just where to go,
Whenever I was feeling low.
I'd take a book down from my memory shelf
And I'd gently turn the pages inside myself.
Now I see you.

Where have you gone, remember me?
It wasn't love, how could it be?
I don't remember ever giving (it) a try,
Took too much for granted and never asked why.
Now I need you, now I need you.

Bridge:
To share some plans, to run, to sing,
And see just where the sun does lead,
Oh, please, I say without regret
That though we were apart,
We learned our lesson well
That love comes from the heart,
That love comes from the heart.

So now you have a place to go,
A simple place, a place to grow
I'll take the book down from my memory shelf
And we'll gently read the pages inside ourselves.
See, I love you (repeat phrase and fade).

She's Like a Lonely Bird

She's like a lonely bird, slowly flying by,
Searching for the one she loves.
She circles round about, now and then she cries,
Calling for the one who left her
With the pain of tears
    Lonely days and fears
Of never, no, never finding love again.

She's like a long child, wandering through the woods,
Trying to find the one she loves.
She searches everywhere, I'd help if I could,
But she just wants the one who left,
She didn't mind the pain
    As long as he remained,
But now, she may never feel his love again.

She's just a lonely girl, holding back the tears,
Waiting for the one she loves.
She's growing older now, harder with the years,
But still she wants the one who left.
She's so all alone,
    She waits till he comes home,
But he, he may never return again.

She's like a lonely bird slowly flying by,
Searching for the one she loves.
I pray she finds him.
I pray she finds him.
I pray she finds him.

Sorry Girl

Sorry girl, but I can never be
The man that you once loved.
Dreaming of him tenderly
While in my arms
Won't bring him back to you
My dear, oh, my love.

Sorry girl, but I just can't exist
Off the love you give to me.
Words of love you whisper in my ear,
But not to me.
How do you think I feel
When you lie to me?

Sorry girl, but I will never be
The man that you once loved.
Learn to dream and learn to love
With me, my dear.
We can make this love worth while.
And live, just love me.
Please love me.
Just love me.

Take Your Hold Off Me

I ask you baby, is love a thing you need?
You think I'm crazy to want to be set free.
But lady, by the morning light
I'll be gone and out of sight.
For I can't give my kind of love
With your hold on me.

Does wanting true love mean watchin' my every move?
Were this a game, love, the way you play you'd lose.
You ask me where I've been all night
And you know that just ain't right.
For you have your time
Like I have mine,
So, take you hold off me.

Chorus:
Take your hold off me, take you hold off me,
I just want to be set free.
Baby, take you hold, take you hold,
Take your hold off me.
I just want to be free.

That's why I ask you baby, is love a thing you need?
For I can love you if you only let me be.
And maybe by the morning light,
You and I will set things right.
I can love you fine
Don't let our love go blind,
Just take your hold off me. (Chorus - then repeat last 3 lines)

Stories

Speak to me softly
    And tell me a story
Of heroes who sailed down a river of gold.
For throughout the ages,
    From fools and ol' sages
Told fairy tales, so I'm told.

Keep me amused
    With the rhymes that they used,
When princes and maidens held love in their hearts.
When wizards would guide them,
    And paupers would hide them
From those who would keep them apart.

    Chorus:
    Carry me onward where stories lie,
    Carry me so far away.
    For in those stories, love never dies,
        The way ours did today.

Stories of rapture
    And love ever after.
When fate was the rule by which men would abide.
And knights who took caution,
    Could find their own fortune
With maidens who rode by their side.

Just keep pretending
    They're all happy endings
With castles, pastures, and cool mountain streams.
Where true love has found them,
    And all that surrounds them
Is better than any could dream. Won't you (chorus)

So (repeat 1st verse and chorus to end.)

Take What You Need and Ride

Bye, bye, bye, bye

Take what you need and ride.
Take what I have, all I offer you.
Take what you need, don't you cry.
It's what you want knowin' I love you.

Chorus I:
Take what you need and ride,
Baby, I'll remember you.
Take what you need and ride,
My love, no one's holdin' you.

Bye, bye, bye, bye

Take what you need and ride.
Take what you want, all I offer you.
Take what you need, don't you cry.
It's only love and what hurt can it do?

Chorus II:
Take what you need and ride,
Baby, I'll remember you.
Take what you need and ride,
But darlin', to thy own self be true.

Bridge:
Just let me hold you hand
Before you cross this land.
The tears in my eyes
As you say good-bye
Bye, bye, bye, bye
Bye -- bye, bye, bye, bye,

(2nd verse and 1st chorus to end.))

Louisianna

It's an old country road and the dust is settlin' down.
A gentle breeze is startin' to blow,
    Just pushin' that dust around.
Bright stars comin' out, small clouds startin' to roam.
A twinkle in my eye, Louisiann, Louisiana I'm comin' home.

Well, I can feel you in the air as you warm my heart within.
Like the hum of a river boat and a touch of southern gin.
I've been everywhere, but every time I looked around,
There you were behind me, Louisiann, Louisiana I'm
    Homeward bound.

Chorus:
Louisiann, you're what I wanna see,
Louisiann, you're such a part of me.
Louisiann, I see you in my eye.
Louisiann, I'll never say goodbye.

Well, the road's 'bout to end, I can see the signs ahead.
I can feel the blood rushin' straight up to my head.
One last look 'round to places I have roamed.
No hard feelings fellas, but Louisiann, Louisiana,
    Your my home.

(Chorus to end.)

Goin' Isn't Easy

When all was said and done that night
He lit a cigarette.
The lady who laid beside him
Talked of things she might forget.
Some music played on the radio
In the corner of the room.
He eyed the ticking clock and thought
It's time for leaving soon.

Chorus I:
Going wasn't easy, going would be hard.
The long and short of a travelin' man
Was an empty, hollowed heart.
Going wasn't easy, going would be hard,
But the road was there before him,
And he had to make a start.

The woman talked of silly things,
She hoped to hide the pain.
She saw that look within his eyes
And heard the midnight train.
A shallow smile came to his lips,
He turned and touched her face.
The music played on through the night
As they made one last embrace.

Chorus II:
Going isn't easy, going can be hard.
The long and short of a travelin' man
Is an empty, hollowed heart.
Going isn't easy, going can be hard,
But the road was there before him,
And he has to make a start.

Bridge:
Time, oh time, time and time again,
The longest he's ever stayed in one place,
He can't remember when.
Time, oh time, time and time again,
There was something always there before him,
Just around the bend.

They stood out by the open door
And looked out on the night.
He felt a chill go through him
As he held the woman tight.
He cleared his throat and softly said,
"Looks like rain."
Then on he walked off (out) in the night
To catch the midnight train.

(Chorus - repeat to end.)

Take Me Home, Girl

Chorus:
Take me home, girl, I don't want to stay,
Good God, I'm bleeding and I need you to find the way.
Take me home, girl, you know I'm gonna die,
I gotta rest a spell, till I see that Kansas sky.

Back in Laredo, for reasons I don't know
She walked into the place.
I was there drinking, sippin' whiskey at the bar.
She walked on up and said, "I know your face."

"It was him!" She screamed to the sheriff behind her.
"It was him!" She was ranting and raving as guns were drawn.
"It was him!" As the air was splintered by shots.
Oh, but I was too slow with my gun,
She stood, watching my blood run. (Chorus)

In desperation, I jumped behind the bar
And got off two quick shots.
She stood standing in that blazing smoke-filled room.
I smashed through the glass, oh, my blood tasted hot.

"It was him!" She screamed - a stray bullet pierced her.
"It was him!" She spilled onto the floor.
"It was him!" The words faded beneath her,
And that's when I told you to run,
Oh ride, baby, ride from those guns. (Chorus)

I shoulda listened when Pa told me to stay.
He said, "Son, why must you go?"
But fame and adventure laid only far away,
Now I can only think of a while ago, the words -

"It was him!" She screamed to the sheriff behind her.
"It was him!" How she laid on the bar room floor.
"It was him!" Why did she choose me?
Cause here I am now, on the run.
Dying from some lawman's gun. (Chorus)

The Audition

Here goes another night
Underneath these staging lights
Auditioning my soul away for you.
Lyrics I memorize.
Some mistakes, can't apologize,
For all I want is to see some dreams come true.
And I enjoy the playing,
Lord, this music keeps me sane,
And I don't mind, I don't mind paying my dues.

Fingers feelin' icy now,
Sweat pourin' down my brow,
For I want is to give a good show for you.
Musicians behind the scenes
Go through cigarettes and magazines
As the tension grows, for we know what we've got to do.
We want to relay a message,
A feelin' of love with each passage;
To give something, to give something of ourselves to you.

Chorus: At the audition (repeat 4 times)

In and out of cafe-bars,
Strummin' song on my sweet guitar
Sometimes the only pay is the pleasure of givin' to you.
Other players do their best
And when we're done, we second-guess
The management, which one of us, they might choose?
Some of us go home sighin',
A few even go home cryin',
For when dreams are shattered what else can one do?

So . . . (repeat 1st verse and chorus to end)

Star

Star of deliverance,
    Lost in the shadow,
Tell me the difference
    B'tween hawk and sparrow.
Don't you know that both can fly,
    Their victims die
        From worm to rabbit, -
The same to the eye.

Star of the morning,
    Leave us an answer.
Give us fair warning,
    From where comes the cancer?
From religious lies?
    Political alibis?
        From the heart of the nation?
It's blinding our eyes.

    Star light, star bright
    First star I see tonight.

Star of redemption
    Or does it really matter?
Mind if I mention
    That I hear the laughter?
Don't you know, 'twas from the skies
    While nations died,
        Just like worms and rabbits.
They fell to the side.

    Star light, star bright
    First star I see tonight. (Repeat and Fade.)

It's You Who I Live For

It's you who I live for,
I'm not gonna change you
Or try to arrange you
To suit only me.

The change people go through
To fool one another,
To make up an image
Through which we can see.

Chorus:
And we'll make our own life.
The changes we'll take in stride.
As long as you're by my side,
Only you, only me.

It's you who I live for
Each day is a memory
Of what we have gone through
To all that can be.

For love's always changing,
Like seasons in nature
And we are love's children
And change constantly.

(Chorus ending with It's you who I live for.)

Love and Peace

Children cry when there is no lovin'.
People cry when no one is there.
Dry your eyes, a season is comin',
When love and peace will flow through the air.

Lullabies sung by a choir,
Voices raised in hopeless despair.
Singing while approaching the hour,
When love and peace will flow through the air.

Chorus:
Let love and peace flow through the air.
Let love and peace flow through the air.
Let love and peace flow through the air.
Let love and peace flow through the air.

What I find that's really so tragic,
Is that people don't seem to care
And so I wait for the evening of magic.
When love and peace will flow through the air.

(Hum and chorus.)

(Repeat 1st verse.)

You 'round here, take a good look around you.
Give me a sign and show me you care.
Take another's hand, it may just astound you,
But let love and peace flow through the air.

(Chorus to end.)

Black Woman's Child

And I, a Black woman' child.

Black woman's child.
Slightly out of time
Inconsistent lullabies
That wouldn't rhyme
Oh those simple, silent hours of our day,
The simple games we played
Like living our lives, living our lives
Our own way

And I, a Black woman's child.

Black woman's child
Whose dreams are planned and made by
Unnecessary lives.
Who never asked him why
His mother gave him love
In the daytime of his life.
Changing darkness into light,
Oh, but what could they know of
A Black woman's love
For her child.

And I, a Black woman's child.

Black woman's child
Touching all the sorrows
That growing has to bring
So sing until tomorrow,

Till the morning finds the dawn
    Sing a soft sweet native song,
For our road is hard and long.
    So touch the souls of your brothers,
Sharing love with one another,
    The love of a Black woman's child;
Ah, the love of a Black woman's child,
Sharing the love of a Black woman's child.
    (Repeat and fade)

Waters Merge With Mine
(Our Wedding Song)

Come and sit by my water's edge.
    Softly tell me that your mine,
Visions making love on some soft bed
    As your waters merge with mine.

Emotions that I seldom share,
    Flowing to you like a stream,
Who'd believe such a love so rare,
    Could make my life seem like a dream.
        Seem like a dream.

  Bridge:
  For down a river you flow
  Toward the shores of my mind.
  The seasons they come and they go
  As your waters merge with mine,
      Waters merge with mine.

Emotions that I seldom share,
    Flowing to you like a stream,
Who'd believe such a love so rare,
    Could make my life seem like a dream.
        Seem like a dream.

*Song I recorded for my wedding, played after our vows.

Other Side of the Sea*

You sail away to distant shores,
You sail away, but not forever;
And while you're gone I'll love you more,
Our love will never die, no never.

And I'll see you when the time is right,
When the stars are bright to guide me
To the other side of the sea.

You knew the time when you would sail,
You smiled and kissed me so completely.
The wind was risin' to a gale,
Your eyes, they said goodbye so sweetly.

And I'll see you when the time is right,
When the stars are bright to guide me
To the other side of the sea.

God speed and God take care,
You're journey's been such a lone one.
A gentle breeze will find you there,
Fragrant air and such a warm sun.

You sail away to distant shores,
You sail away, but not forever;
And while you're gone I'll love you more,
Our love will never die, no never.

And I'll see you when the time is right,
When the stars are bright to guide me
To the other side of the sea.

*My mother nearly died from a brain aneurysm when I wrote this for her. Fortunately, she survived. Eighteen years later I performed it at her funeral with my close friend, Donn Lowe.

How Much Longer Can We Ride?

How much longer can we ride,
    Before the engine fails?
I feel the chase not far behind,
    I hear the sirens wail.

This situation calls for speed,
    So ride, ride for goodness sake.
Stop tellin' me what you need,
    Just don't make the same mistakes!

    Your hesitation,
        speculation
            is makin' it hard to move.
    Stop analyzin',
        start energizin'
            we can make it baby, we just got to be cool.

    How much longer can we ride?
    How much longer can we ride?
    How much longer can we ride?
    How much longer can we rider?

Just keep the rhythm goin' strong.
    You've got to keep the faith.
Hold, yeah, keep holdin' on,
    I can still feel the chase.

Head for the sun that's risin' high,
I've got to feel the light.
Look, look who's after us,
It's only you and I,

Your hesitation,
speculation
is makin' it hard to move.
Stop analyzin',
start energizin'
we can make it baby, we just got to be cool.

How much longer can we ride?
How much longer can we ride?
How much longer can we ride?
How much longer can we rider?

Golden Days

First voice:
In the light of day,

Second voice:
Neath the morning sun.

First voice:
Children on parade,

Second voice:
I'm the lonely one.

Both voices:
Carry me on pass the golden gates,
Tell me my first mistake.

First voice:
Children tell me please,

Second voice:
Take me by the hand,

First voice:
I'm too blind to see.

Second voice:
Can't you understand?

Both voices:
In the dark, ever my eyes will be.
What can this mean for me?

> Am I too old for a rhyme?
> Am I still free in my mind
> Or am I closed.

First voice:
Children on parade,

Second voice:
Kindly rescue me,

First voice:
With the games you play,

Second voice:
Come and set me free.

Both voices:
Take my hand and lead me far away,
Back to my golden days.

Sun Overdue

One summer morning, the sun was overdue
The children's courtyard was covered by the dew
Who waits for sunlight to filter out the rain,
And brighten faces of our children again.

A season changes when what was can be no more.
A constant rainfall has kept our kids indoors.
Within their own world, they play a game or two,
And wait for sunlight which is long over due.

Bridge:
The empty seasons of a lonely Black child,
Pathetic reasons as to why he(she) should smile.
There's no sun in the sky, so he(she) must rely
    on memories,
        oh those old memories.

And in the distance where our children rarely play,
Far past the dark clouds and the dew in shades of gray
One star shines brightly on the faces of the young
I hear them calling "Come and see everyone.
We can see the sun, or how we see the sun.
    A sun so long over due."

Children, What Do They Know That We Don't?

Singers sing of peace,
Trouble in the land,
Children by a waterfall
Play games and holding hands.
Shadows fill the halls,
Beware the judgment day,
Missiles sailing through the sky
And still the children play.

What do they know that we don't?
Why can't we see through their eyes?
What did we lose by playing by the rules?
We need to open up our eyes,
I said, "Open up our eyes."

Violence on the screen,
Tension in the air,
Children sucking lemon drops,
Engaged in bedtime prayer.
Hunger takes its toll
As babies cease to cry,
Children ask their mom and dad,
"Is Heaven in the sky?"

What do they know that we don't?
Why can't we see through their eyes?
What did we lose by playing by the rules?
We need to open up our eyes,
I said, "Open up our eyes."

Seekers of the truth,
Lost in your charade,
Listen to the laughter dance
As children promenade.
Gather one and all,
Wherever you may be.
Remember, it was wisely said,
"In Heaven such are these."

What do they know that we don't?
Why can't we see through their eyes?
What did we lose by playing by the rules?
We need to open up our eyes,
I said, "Open up our eyes."

What's a Friend For?
(Written with Glenn Spivack)

Well, if life is a scuffle,
    Could I trust you at my back?
Would you watch that door behind me
    Or would you open it, just a crack?
If love was measured in units,
    And I needed 'bout a dime,
Would you tell me, "I'm so sorry,
    But I haven't got the time?"

    Chorus:
    Who takes the weight
        When your friends give you the load?
    And who will want your overcoat
        When the winds blow strong and cold?
    What's a friend, what's a friend, what's a friend for?

If my engine rolled on over,
    And fell right off the tracks.
Would you help me get it started,
    Or laugh as I broke my back?
And if you had a huge mess of beans,
    And I gave you an empty plate.
Would you say, "Your eyes may shine,
    Your teeth may grit, but you're a little bit too late.

    Chorus:

And if I were dangling from a high place,
    And you had a long strong rope,
Would you cut it into pieces, saying,
    "Brother, I just can't cope."
Hey, if living depends on breathing
    And you had all the air,
Would you give me a tank of carbon monoxide, sayin'
    "Here's your share."

Chorus to end.

Everybody Wants

Everybody wants a place in the sky,
Everybody wants to make it on through.
And everybody would love a piece of the pie,
But nobody wants to pay their dues.

Everybody wants to get things for free,
Everybody wants to eat their own cake,
And everyone would like a life-time guarantee
That this ol' body will never wear, tear or break.

Chorus:
Hear the bells toll,
Only you know who you are.
See the rainbow,
Tell me what you owe this world so far,
Caste you shadow
Straight and narrow, touch a, touch a star.

Everybody wants to be first in line,
Everybody wants to be number one
And all of you want peace in our times,
But nobody wants to put down their gun.

Chorus:

Everybody wants it all out in front,
Yet everybody wants it where no one can see.
All of you, you know what you want,
But do you really know what you need?

Chorus:

Everybody wants a place in the sky,
Everybody wants to make it on through.
And everybody would love a piece of the pie,
But nobody wants to pay their dues.

Like I said - chorus

One Within One

I'd like to tell you, I'd like to show you,
I'd like to give you and come to know you.
I'd like to find you, I want to hold you
And let you rest in my arms.
I'd like to touch you, if only for a little while
And let you know that we are one.

Chorus:
For there's more to this than meets the eye,
There's more to this, if you look inside,
There's more to this, you will realize
We are one within one within one.

I'd like to sing to you, I'd like to reach you.
I want to learn from you, I'd like to teach you,
To come and care for you and be there for you
When you feel you're the only one.
For when I'm with you, I'm with myself,
As the truth to all will come.

Chorus:

I'd like you to tell me, I'd like you to show me,
I'd like you to give me, and come to know me.
I'd like you to find me, I want you to hold me
And let me rest in your arms.
I'd like you to touch me if only for a little while
And let me know that we are one.

Chorus:

If Ever I Needed You (I Need You Now)

You said you'd love me forever,
You said you'd never leave my side.
But that's when times were happy.
When everything seemed fine
And promises were a dozen a dime.

Hey baby, where are you goin'?
I know these past months have been kind of hard.
Oh, but I've been tryin'.
As much as time would allow,
And I thought, I thought you knew by now.

Chorus:
If ever, if ever I needed you,
I need you now.

You know I'm goin' to ask you not to leave me,
But that's not what this is all about.
You're talkin' about finding treasure,
I'm talkin' about dodgin' clouds,
Cause I now we can make it somehow (chorus)

Bridge:
Just be real for the moment,
You know that life isn't easy.
It's smooth and it's hard,
And when it's hard
You've got to hold on, hold on, hold, hold on, hold on,
For cryin' out loud (chorus)

Oh, but I've been tryin'
As much as time would allow.
Cause I know we can make it somehow. (Chorus to end.)

Bye, Bye, Baby

You can believe what you will,
I don't understand how you can listen
to all those lies.
What about my side?
Well, if you're gonna believe those crazy lies.
Well, then it's bye, bye, baby, baby,
bye, bye, baby, baby, baby, bye, bye.

What do you be doin' all day?
Waitin' by the phone for some useless
information on my every move.
Ooh, girl, I'm so proud of you.
In fact, one day I might just drop you a line -
Sayin; bye, bye, baby, baby,
bye, bye, baby, baby, baby, bye, bye

Bridge:
You can believe what you want.
I ain't doing nothin' wrong.
It's all in your mind.
You'd be thinkin' I'm double-timin'
When I speak, you think I'm lyin'
I'm tired of tryin', well, it's bye, bye, baby, baby,
bye, bye, baby, baby, baby, bye, bye.

You're acting like the CIA.
Lurking in the shadows, watching every
little move I make.
Ooh, girl that's your big mistake,
Cause if you're gonna play the part of a spy -
Well, then it's bye, bye, baby, baby,
bye, bye, baby, baby, baby, bye, bye
(Repeat bridge and go out on "bye, bye.")

Considerin' (Livin' for Today)

Considerin' what it's worth, I think I'll try to travel on.
Livin' off the earth, like some lowly vagabond.
And though I don't show what I feel.
Sometimes the road is all too real.
Livin' for today off the music that I play.
Off the music that I play,
Off the music that I play.

Rollin' in through towns on the wheels of poverty.
Stayin' long enough to become a novelty,
And then it's back along the road -
I want to share this crazy load.
Livin' for today off the music that I play.
Off the music that I play.
Off the music that I play.

Bridge:
Oh home, where have you gone to?
Considerin' what it's worth too, I'd better travel on.
Ooh, you, please don't remind me,
And don't try to find me, I'm not where I belong.

(Repeat 1st verse.)

Better Stay Here (Till the Morning)

Oh, I know that you got your problems,
But baby, don't you know that I got mine.
Don't we all carry a burden
Up a hill that's so hard to climb.
And you can say your load is heavier than mine.
Well, if that's so, then share your load with me.
And we can surely try,
Try to find the reasons why,
But it may take some time.

Chorus:
Better stay here till the morning.
Better stay here through the night.
Better stay here till the morning,
Till we can work it out,
Till we can work it out,
We can work it out right.,

Just because some of your bridges
And some of your castles have turned to sand.
Don't give up, someone will guide you,
Someone is there, just reach out your hand.
Oh, you can swear you've heard this same ol' line before,
And you've yet to see an open door.
Well, mine stands open wide,
So in me confide,
But it may take some time. (Chorus)

(Repeat last half of 1st verse and chorus to end.)

Excuses, Excuses

Another day, another life-time,
Tomorrow waits, so, put off things that you need.
Whose mouth ya gonna feed?
One reason why we can't accept change.
We spend our time playing ego games on you,
And you be playing too.

Chorus:
First you say you need a break,
People say you're born too late.
So, you take it from the man.
Find out you've been running hard,
You can only go so far.
Catch me if you can,
Ah, nah, nah, nah, ...Excuses (repeat)

Too old to fight, too young to deal with,
The stars aren't right, they say you should stay home.
Leave this day alone.
No need to take such risky chances,
Just let the work of Fate arrange things for you.
Who gives a damn what you do? (Chorus)

You'd rather sit and watch parades pass.
While years of dust lay on your naked dreams,
Rusty, broken dreams.
But you feel safe, time's in your pocket,
Within your reach, you just have to say the word.
Silly little word. (Chorus to end.)

In the Streets of the City

I love to walk the streets of town,
Good lookin' women all around.
For a traveler who's been alone,
You make this boy feel right at home.

Chorus I:
Ooh, la, la. You're lookin' good today.
No, nah, nah, nah. Don't send this boy away.
Ooh, baby, babe, Come on over here.
Ooh, yah, yah, yah. Well, alright,
Give me some sugar.

Been on the road, I need a rest.
Playin' games at people's request.
Good night's lovin' is all I need,
Just name the place, I'll follow, you lead.

Chorus II:
Ooh, la, la. You're lookin' good today.
No, nah, nah, nah. Don't send this boy away.
Ooh, baby, babe, Come on over here.
Ooh, yah, yah, yah. Well, alright,
Now Mama, do it, do it.

Bridge:
Ooh, la, la. In the streets of the city.
Ooh, la, la. la. The women so, so pretty.
Ooh, la, la. In the streets of the city.
Ooh, la, la. la. The women so, so pretty.

(Repeat 1st verse, 1st and 2nd chorus, ending with bridge.)

Saturday Nights

Saturday evenings,
Can't wait till it comes around.
Cause every weekend,
That's when my baby comes to town.

We're gonna turn the lights down low,
We're gonna do it real slow,
So, I'm savin' all my love for Saturday nights

Just   ' here dreamin'.
Wanna share my thoughts with you,
Plannin' and schemin'.
Ooh, girl, what I'm gonna do for you.

We're gonna take it nice and easy,
I wanna feel you hug and squeeze me,
So, I'm savin' all my love for Saturday nights.

Chorus:
Oh-oh girl, I really need you,
This waiting makes me, makes me, makes me wanna,
Oo-ooh, girl.
I -- I, I wanna love and hold you,
Just like I told you,
I wanna let you know that you'll
Always be mine.

(Repeat last part of 2nd verse, chorus and end with 1st verse.)

Wars in Those Days

Shortly ere the gods began to fall,
Sea winds raged havoc through the halls
Of temples entrenched in mountain sides.
And as demons began to rise,
Pagans in tear-stained eyes, gazed toward heaven.

Chorus:
Wars in those days,
Were caused when gods raged
Across the open skies
While men of flesh were dying.

Lightning, the answer to their gaze.
Thunder of bitter gods enraged.
And madness had plagued the holy land,
As a prophet in sinking sand,
Heals with a bloody hand, those who die swearin'.
(Chorus I:)

Eons and all the gods have fled,
Heaven, a place to send your dead.
And mankind has changed the holy land
To a mound where no man can stand,
Less he have gun in hand, to kill all intruders.

Chorus II:
Wars in these days,
Are caused when men rage
Across the open sky,
Tomorrow's children dying.

Makin' Love

Chorus:
There's nothin' in the takin'
But there's somethin' in the makin'
Of makin' love, makin' love, makin' love,
Makin' love, makin' love, makin' love, makin' love.

I feel kind of wonderful, now that I know what givin'
Is all about.
I ain't scared any more. I feel your love and I just wanna shout.
As long as you feel what is real, don't hesitate.
Don't ever wait to give your heart.
Learn, learn from the learned.
Take a chance and make a brand new start. Cause (chorus)

I used to think I was satisfied, takin' love from
Whoever came my way.
Then I met a fine, sweet woman, who gave me more than
I could ever take.
Found myself givin', livin', makin', creatin', awakin',
And sayin' that (chorus)

Bridge:
I just wanna tell how you happy givin' makes me feel,
And even if my heart gets broken,
I'll know what I gave was real, ohh (chorus)

(Repeat 1st verse and go out on chorus.)

The Best Love

Two more seasons, passed and gone,
 And my love, no one can find.
So very hard to carry on
 In the same frame of mind.

But I remember her words to me
 Whenever I felt bad.
"Of all the loves that I have known,
 You're the best one that I've had."
She said, "Of all the loves that I have known,
 You're the best one that I've had."

Empty days with empty friends,
 Who don't know how I feel.
Plastic love that never ends,
 You know it don't seem real.

Still, I remember her words to me
 Which alway made me glad.
"Of all the loves that I have known,
 You're the best one that I've had."
She said, "Of all the loves that I have known,
 You're the best one that I've had."

Bridge:
And there were times you would call on me
 To always hold you near.
And then one day you changed your life-style
 Which brought on all my fears.

Woke one morning and found you'd gone,
    With a letter of pain in my hand.
Your written word of the tears I caused,
    For reasons I don't understand

But I remember the good times
    And if it's you who's feeling bad.
"Well, all the loves I have known,
    You're the best one that I've had."
"Of all the loves that I have known,
    You're the best one that I've had."

(Repeat last two lines 3x.)

Two Are Never Alone

First voice: Second voice:

Sitting in my room,
Feel the walls closing in,
Waiting for these tears to dry
.
Once again I lose.
How many loves has it been?
How many times must I try?

Chorus (both voices)
Two are never alone.
Two are never alone.
Two are never alone.
One must have another,
Depending on each other.

Hours drifting by
No one calls, no one cares.
Silence is my only company.

When she (he) said goodbye,
Lost the years that we shared.
How can I survive? Tell me.
For now, I need someone to hold me, hold me. (Chorus)

Yet, I know inside,
It won't take very long.
Someone down the road waits patiently.
And when I see her (his) eyes
We will know we belong.
Love is on its way to me.
For we know loneliness can hurt you, hurt you.
(Chorus -- repeat and fade)

Better Times, Better Days
(Written with Keith Gonzales)

Better times, better days,
Better dreams are comin'
Don't start running away.
Tis the season,
Find your reason for life.
Make the journey,
Don't you worry, I'm by your side.

Bridge:
The light of morning is in your eyes,
So take the time to make this day your day!
Just see the magic and you'll realize
That everything is gonna come your way.

Better times, better days,
Make your morning brighter
Load 'lot lighter today.
Hear the laughter?
Just who's the master of your life?
Take my hand,
We'll make a stand, I'm by your side.

(Bridge, 2nd verse and fade with better times, better days.)

Dream Lady

There was a dream drifting by,
And it gently settled to my side.
It touched my soul and I fell in.
I saw the lady of my day-dream,
Running through meadows and touching clouds.
In amongst the sounds that softly descended from Heaven.
And she glanced my way.

Chorus:
Dream lady, I see you, can't believe my eyes.
Dream woman, forever, are you really mine? (Repeat)

In a trance, in a dream,
I heard a silent stream
Of caressing words from her gentle voice.
The mist then cleared and she was near me.
Gazing at me as only a goddess could.
Touching my hand, we went to a garden in Eden,
Where we found ourselves.

Bridge:
Dream Lady, I find you wanting me.
Can it be that I'll never touch your cloud?

And as the evening filled the sky,
My love nestled by my side.
Yeah, she whispered things that I should know.
That with the morning she must leave me.
And search the heavens to find my star.
Cherish it deeply and maybe this dream will last forever.
Then she'll come to me.
My dream lady

(Repeat chorus, fading with "my dream lady.")

Stormy Weather

Stormy weather
Coming after me.
Seasons changing.
Oh Lord, can this really be?
Got to keep on ridin',
Got to keep on movin' on
Toward sunlight, toward sunlight.

Bridge:
Forecast says, babe, it's gonna rain,
Got to move on, can't stand the pain.
Got to ride this storm in my mind, babe.
'Fore the rain starts pourin' down,
Pourin' down, pourin' down, pourin' down.

(Repeat 1st and bridge.)

Be There

Someday, you said that I will understand.
And while you sit there holding another's hand,
That day seems far away.

Sometime, you said you would need me again.
But if to need should mean you'd leave again,
It's best you change your mind.

Bridge:
And so you expect me to wait around,
After all the times you tried to bring me down.
Nah, Nah, nah, nah, - - - - -

"Be there," you said, before you walked away.
And I say, "Sorry baby, but I cannot stay,
For I found someone who cares,
Really cares."

I'll Never Leave Again

Ah, the rain,
Pourin' from the sky,
And the pain,
Makes you close your eyes.

Chorus I:
It's all right,
Just hold tight,
I'll never leave again.

You and I
Have been through so, so much.
If we try,
We can learn, learn to touch.

Chorus II:
It's all right,
Just hold tight,
I'll never leave again, never again.

(Lead and chorus)

See the sun
Shining in the sky.
My love one,
Open your sweet brown eyes.

(Chorus II and chorus I to end.)

Wine and Beer

Hey you, sitting in the corner.
Hmm, do you wanna
 Meet someone tonight?
I understand, you've got your suspicions,
A woman's intuition.
 Don't worry, I won't bite.

 Chorus I:
 Oh and I, I've been watchin' you for quite some time.
 Each night, since you've been comin' here.
 May I, may I order you a glass of wine?
 Hey Charlie, yeah, and bring me a beer.

Should we talk or get on the dance floor?
Ooh, yeah, let me see you smile more,
 It really brightens up your eyes.
You say you like my songs, you like my music.
Thanks, I intend to pursue it.
 Yeah, I'm aiming for the skies.

 Chorus II:
 Oh and I, I've been watchin' you for quite some time,
 Each night, since you've been comin' here.
 Hey Charlie, could you move it with that glass of wine.
 Oh yeah, don't forget my beer.

Bridge:
Ooh, where are you gonna go?
Ooh, what are you gonna do,
 Now that the show is through?
Hmm, well I just wanna know,
Cause I, I wanna spend some time with you.

Hey you, sitting neath a rainbow,
I love the way your eyes glow.
    What say we find a hideaway?
You say you got a place, just around the corner.
You're askin' if I wanna,
    Leave here right away.

    Chorus III:
    After I, I been watchin' you for quite some time,
    Each night, since you've been comin' here.
    Hey Charlie, why don't you hold that glass of wine,
        And chase it with that beer.
    I said, hey Charlie, why don't you hold that glass of wine
        And chase it with that beer.
    I'm gettin' out of here, gettin' out of here.

If I Only Had the Time

If I only had the time,
You know, I've heard that line before.
If I only had the time,
I'd turn my life around
And really try to score.

If I only had a chance,
Is what so many people say.
If I only had a chance
I could have made it big,
My name would have lit up Broadway.

Bridge I:
But I was too busy paying my bills
And trying to stay alive.
I was so secure eating a meal,
And doing my nine-to-five.
So little did I realize
That time was passing by,
And so the years kept on rolling,
My chances were going
At keeping my dreams alive.
Now I'm pushing seventy-five.

(Repeat 1st verse.)

If I knew what I know now,
An ol' man's poor excuse.
If I knew what I know now,
I would have gave my all.
I would have paid up all my dues.

Bridge II:
But I was too busy doing things
  I never meant to do.
It was so easy turning away
  From something I had to pursue.
So little did I realize
That I was being screwed.
And as the years kept on rolling
My chances were going
At keeping my point of view,
Keeping my point of view.
Now I'm pushing eighty-two.

(Repeat 1st verse)

If I only had contacts,
That ol' familiar phrase.
If I only had contacts,
This song would be a hit,
And I'd be sittin' back for days.

Bridge III:
But I was too busy paying my bills
  And trying to stay alive.
I was so secure eating a meal
  When my pension check would arrive.
So little did I realize
That time was passing by,
And as the years kept on rolling
My chances were going
At keeping my dreams alive.
Now I'm pushing ninety-five. (Repeat 1st verse and end)

Rosie*

Rose, Heaven should see you smile,
Come, let us love awhile, be mine.

Surely I will come for you,
Surely there's a place for us to be.
Gently place your hand in mine, any time.
Come with me.
Your love brightens every moment,
Giving all and assuring dreams constantly.

Rosie, sunlight is in your eyes,
Sing me a lullaby, be mine.

Like a songbird in the sky, starry eyed,
You come to me.
Gently spoken words of love
As we lay here quietly.
Feel free to take my heart away, baby,
Hold me tight, let's give this night memories.

Rosie, Heaven should see you smile.

*While I wrote many songs to my wife, this one held her name. She has a winning smile.

Sally West

Sally West, shoutin' to the people,
Knowin' she could never belong.
At her best, talkin' 'bout her sufferin'
And them suckers that done her wrong.
She could fly, riding on the subways,
Stinking up the IND.
An evil eye, she gives to every passerby,
"Why ya keep lookin' at me?"

Chorus:
Shove it! Stick in your ear!
Stick it where the sun don't shine!
Just stick it in any ol' hole,
As long as that hole ain't mine!

Sally West, found on every corner.
Every corner where the news is bad.
So depressed, counting her possessions
Found in every shopping bag.
Never begs, nah, she wants nothin';
Not even the time of day.
Once a preacher gave her a dollar bill
And I distinctly heard her say, (chorus)

Sally West, you can find her in midtown,
Talkin' 'bout payin' dues.
At her best bleedin' her heart out,
Talkin' 'bout being abused.
There she goes, movin' to the rhythm
Of the city's darker side.
And at a corner a boy pokes fun
And you can hear ol' Sally cry, (chorus, repeat)

Runaway Train

Well, the beat was grovin',
The party was movin'.
Whole lotta shakin' goin' on.
Yeah, the bass lines were burnin',
The tables were turnin'.
That party upstairs was rockin' on.

I'm downstairs in my apartment,
Sleeping off that jive nine-to-five,
But the walls all around me were rockin' thin.
Yeah, the place was 'bout to blow sky high.

Chorus:
It was like a runaway train,
Twistin' and turnin',
That disco comin' through the floor.
It was like a runaway train,
Where's the conductor?
I don't think I can take anymore.

I went in my Pee Jay's
To speak to the DeeJay.
To ask him, could he slow down a bit.
But the hallway was smokin'
From some things they were rollin'
Someone said, "Here, take a whiff."

By the time that I got the next flight,
I felt like engine no. 9.
I found myself blowin' some whistle, sayin'.
"Don't stop till the end of the line!"

Chorus (same except for last line.)
Now what did I come here for?

Bridge:
Runaway train, ka-choo, ka-choo,
ka-choo, whoo-whoo. whoo-whoo.
Runaway train, ka-choo, ka-choo,
ka-choo, whoo-whoo. whoo-whoo.

Well, the beat was grovin',
The party was movin'.
Whole lotta shakin' goin' on.
Yeah, the bass lines were burnin',
The tables were turnin'.
I knew this was the place I belonged.

I was there la-freakin' in my Pee Jays,
Hustlin' in my bedroom shoes,
Someone said, "Next stop is Funksville,
So get down on this ol' choo-choo.

Chorus - (same except for last line.)
Give me more, give me more, give me more (repeat)

(Bridge: repeat and fade.)

Crystal Mountain Morning
(Written with Donn Lowe)

Chorus:
All rise, it's a crystal mountain morning.
Sunlight is comin' overhead.
Nearby the waters ever flowing.
Meet you by the riverbed.

Last night we camped beneath the stars.
By firelight we told ol' stories.
Hours passed just playing our guitars
Till dawn approached in all its glory.

Free, oh so free,
Free. Free to find peace of mind. (Chorus)

The mountain pine on such a pretty day.
Fills my mind and frees my spirit.
The water's great, let's take a swim today.
This forest land, I love to be near it.

Free, oh so free,
Free. Free to find peace of mind. (Chorus)

Do You Really Want Me to Leave?

You and I got to work things out,
I don't like the fighting and the doubt,
You say you know what this romance is coming to.
Well, so do I, the message is comin' through

Chorus:
Do you really want me to leave?
Do you thinks that our lives would be better?
You were hinting at this in a letter
Two months ago.
Well, baby, I disagree.
Don't you know that I feel we can make it.
If we keep it real and don't fake it,
Then love can grow.

You and I can't let it fall apart.
I don't know all the secrets in your heart.
I only know that leavin' won't solve a thing.
Ooh, I love you. To me you're everything. (Chorus)

Bridge:
You know there was a time
When, oh, how our love would shine.
Love had made us blind.
All in one day.
I just can't reveal
All the things you made me feel.
Lovin' you is real.
Don't send me away. (Chorus)

(2nd half of 2nd verse and chorus to end.)

The End of the Dream

Sunlight came creeping in this morning,
Time passes quickly so it seems.
A while ago we were in heaven.
Now it's the end of the dream.

Our love was warm and oh, so tender.
But rays of sun fell in between
The tears when you tried to tell me.
"This is the end of the dream."

Chorus:
And I cried, "Why, why, oh why,
Must the morning come?
It was you, not I
Who called the morning sun!"
Paradise faded before me,
The love we had was gone,
It was the end of the dream.

We walked the paths of heaven.
Kissed by many golden streams.
But with the sun my eyes were opened.
It was the end of the dream.

(Repeat 1st verse and chorus to end.)

Our Love

Trees are only trees
Until one stands beneath the shade.
And feels the beauty,
    Feels the beauty
Of life's unchanging scheme.
And the mystery of it all.
Oh, I wonder how our love is like a tree?

Land is only land,
You learn to take and give to it,
And feel the power,
    Feel the power.
From a simple lump of clay,
The world had once began.
Oh, I wonder how our love is like the land?

    Chorus:
    Oh, it's so strange
    How my eyes view the world,
    Looking through the world --
    Each glance makes the music revolve.

(Break and chorus)

We are only we,
But place love in the midst of us
And feel the glory.
    Feel the glory
Of love's awakening,
Ooh, the magic in the air
And the knowledge that our love is more than we,
    More than we, more than we.

I Love You

This song seems the same,
Like something I've heard before.
The chord structure still retains,
The echoes of some troubadour.

But it sounds so appropriate
For something I want to say,
It sounds kind of musical,
You know you make me feel that way.

Chorus:
Oh I, I-I, I love you.

Those words are in every song,
In every poem with a rhyme,
In every painting on a wall,
In every age, in every time.

But no three words in all the world
Have power to combine.
It's the truth of life itself.
Like the love you share with mine. (Chorus)

Bridge:
There's no illusion in reality,
I only have to know what's real.
It's not this song and it's not the words,
It's in the love, it's in the love.
It's in the love that I feel, that I feel.

This song seems the same,
Like something I've heard before.
Maybe someone knows the name,
Maybe someone knows the score

But it sounds so appropriate
For something I want to say,
The three words in all the world
That says what I feel today. (Chorus)

The Performer

They all came to hear him play.
They all came believin'
He could chase the clouds away,
Set their minds to dreamin'.

They knew the words to every song,
Some even sang along.
It made them fell like they belonged,
If only for the evenin'.

Chorus:
Oh, they say he could satisfy,
Touch your heart with a sweet ol' lullaby.

There'd be a story he could tell,
That was food for consolin'.
He's change the tune and they would yell
When he was rock-n-rollin'.

A light would break on through the clouds,
High, he could take the crowd.
And through the night they sang aloud,
"Just take us where you're goin'." (chorus)

Bridge:
And if you feel that no one really cares,
He can give you hope where there was none.
And should you have somebody with you there,
He can make the two of you feel as one, yeah.

They all came to hear him play.
The all came believin'
    He could chase the clouds away,
Set their minds to dreamin'.

They all stay on through the night,
Glad he had shown the light,
They say he was out of sight,
Really had them screamin'.

(Chorus - repeat to end.)

Run, Michael, Run

Is anybody going to the market,
  Going to the market,
  Going to the market place?
Do you know Charlie's Fruit Stand
  Owned by a huge man
  With razor tracks all over his face?
In the back there's a young guy
  Only has one good eye,
  Dealin' with the cartons and crates.
Could you tell him, tell him for me

  Chorus I:
  Say, "Michael, boy you better run,
  Cause Paula's Papa's comin'
  And the rumors keep-a-hummin'
  He's a crazy man, packin' a gun."
  Tell him, Michael, Michael, Mike you better,
    Run, run, run, run, run, run, run.

Come on and do this one favor.
  Do this one favor,
  Do this one favor for me.
But before you go a callin'
  Let me give fair warnin',
  Mike's as crazy as crazy can be.
He's touchy and he's mean,
  The reddest eye you've ever seen,
  Make you wonder can he really see.
So be easy when you tell him for me,

Chorus I:
Say, "Michael, boy you better run,
Cause Paula's Papa's comin'
And let me tell you something,
You ain't no match for a gun."
Tell him, Michael, Michael, Mike you better,
Run, run, run, run, run, run, run.

Tell him, Paula went in labor,
Paula went in labor,
Paula went in labor today.
I would have told you sooner
But she called him Mikey junior.
And kind-a gave the secret away.
Now Paula's Papa knows,
Hey Mick, you better go
Cause he intends to blow you away.
Tell him Michael, listen to me (Chorus I)

So if you're going to the market,
Going to the market,
Going to the market place.
Go to Charlie's Fruit Stand
Owned by a huge man
With razor tracks all over his face.
In the back you tell Michael
To get his motorcycle,
And get the hell out of that place. (Chorus II)

Rockin' and Rollin' (Till the Break of Dawn)

I can tell this ain't my kind of work,
I can tell this ain't my gig.
Been pushin' papers far too long.
Something gotta give.
Cause deep within my heart, yeah mama,
I can hear a song,
Rockin' and Rollin'
Gettin' down, till the break of dawn.

Understand, there's no better love
Than my sweet guitar.
Everyday I dreams a lot,
Bout being a star.
Oh, I can hear those people screamin',
There ain't nothin' wrong,
With rockin' and rollin',
Gettin' down, till the break of dawn.

Got to leave this nine to five,
Got to spread my wings.
Only way to stay alive
Is to do my thing.
Cause deep within my heart, yeah mama,
That's where I belong,
Rockin' and Rollin'
Gettin' down, till the break of dawn.

Song Lyrics
from
1981 to 1990.

Love Comes Alive

Walkin' the streets all alone.
With no place to go to.
Sadness goes, straight to the bone,
You stumble in the night.
You feel like you're 'bout to explode.
It burns deep inside you.
You say, "Hold on, hold on.
It'll be alright."

The shadows of yesterday's dreams
Still come to haunt you.
Feelin' the pain as you go,
The tears fill up your eyes.
Friends try to lessen your fears.
The always remind you,
They say, "Hold on, hold on.
It'll be alright."

Chorus:
No one knows just when true love will find you.
No one knows the where, the how, the why --
But just when you feel you're lost,
With no star to guide you.
Love, sweet love comes alive.

Bridge:
You've got to, you've got to hold on,
Love will come again.
You pray it won't take very long,
Cause there's pain in waiting.
It might come today, tomorrow, sometime,
But you've got to believe love comes alive. (Chorus)

(Repeat 1st verse and chorus to end.)

Love Ist

Love, don't be afraid to love,
For there's so much more in the giving of
Believe, it may be hard to see,
But love is giving more than you receive.

Care, some say it's hard to care,
But there's a need for someone there.
And we must learn to fill the need,
For love is giving more than you receive.

And in time, our light will shine
Brighter than all the stars in the sky.
Oh just love.

True love means giving more than you receive.

And in time, our light will shine
Brighter than all the stars in the sky.
If we only love.

Don't be afraid to love,
For there's so much more in the giving of
And we must learn to fill the need,
For love is giving more,
True love is giving more than you receive.

Help Me Out‡

I'm deep in the water Lord
And you know I can't swim.
Send someone to rescue me
From this trouble that I'm in.

Chorus I:
Hard times lookin' for me,
Of that there's no doubt.
Good God, help me, help me out!

Now I'm not much for praying,
Then again I'm not much for pain.
And when I feel forsaken Lord
I call upon your name.

Chorus II:
I'm takin' in water,
Goin' down for the count.
Good God, help me, help me, help me out!

Bridge:
I don't want to tell you how to do your job
With so many people suffering out loud.
But just a little sympathy
Would go a long, long way for me.

I'm deep in the water Lord
And you know I can't swim.
Send someone to rescue me
From this trouble that I'm in.

(Chorus II -- repeat "help me!" to end.)

The Way of Things‡

I still remember
The way it use to be,
The lovin'.
Everywhere I turn I see you and me
Holdin' on.

Chorus:
We knew it in our hearts,
Felt it in our dreams.
Swore we'd never part,
It's just the way of things.

I can still hear
The trembling in your voice.
Not knowing.
It just seems so unreal to say there was no choice
In moving on. (Chorus)

Bridge:
Your love was mine.
There's no way I could forget.
But passing time
Fills me with regrets.

Sometimes I wonder,
Do you think of me
With yearning?
Choices that we make
Unable to foresee
Losing all. (Chorus to end)

I Am Self

Chorus:
I am Self, yes Self,
The One Supreme Being.
I am Self, yes Self,
So whom shall I fear?
I am Self, yes Self,
Self is the strength of my life,
Self is the strength of my life.
So, whom shall I fear?

Some (most) people out there don't know what it means.
When I tell them, I'm a neti - neti being.
They try to tell I'm only human.
I say, "I'm more than that,
Much more than, I know who I am." (Chorus)

Khaibit all around, most people can't escape.
Satipatthana helps to liberate,
I slow my breathing - Dhyana come with ease
And as I meditate,
Yes meditate, samadhi sows the seed, that (chorus)

The years behind me, I'm putting to the side,
To clean this temple, so Self can abide.
To know my proper role is the best means of defense.
The one who's uninvolved,
Yes uninvolved, the Willer of events.
That's my Self . . . (chorus to end.)

What a Lovely Way to Go

I picked up my winnings last night,
    Everything was going all right.
I walked up to the bar,
    Put down my guitar.
Said, "Give me something mellow and nice."
Drank it down, nice and slow,
    Felt the fire burnin' down below.
Ahh, what a lovely, lovely, lovely why to go.

Drove my Chevy to the nearest star,
    Who cares, I never got that far.
Just cruisin' through the night,
    Veering to the right,
Puffing an ol' cigar.
Yeah, ridin' to feel the flow,
    Rockin' to some rock n' roll,
Ooh, what a lovely, lovely, lovely way to go.

Bridge:
When I got home, she was waiting
    In the back room shoutin' something.
"Come on, let me take you higher,
    Let me set your soul on fire."
I felt the heat, I knew defeat.
    I couldn't quit, cause this was it.
Ahh, what a lovely, lovely , lovely way to go.

(Break - ending with "What a lovely way to go.")

We were lovin' to the edge of the night.
    It was something that was out of sight.
There was magic in the air,
    Fire everywhere.
Lovin' her keeps me alive.
Yeah, she's worth her weight in gold,
    Feel so good, don't you know.
Ooh, what a lovely, lovely, lovely way to go. (Repeat 3x to end)

The Hero

In my boyhood fables
    a hero was always able
Upon his trusty steed
    to arrive in the nick of time.

The hero was always after
    a damsel so near disaster.
One always knew his honor
    Would save her from the crime.

    Oh, what a hero's life could be,
        You see,
    For if I were a hero,
        You'd be loving me.

Heroes take all the chances
    and many more romances,
Willing to gamble
    and rarely ever lose.

In my favorite story,
    I would win all the glory.
You'd see my greatness
    and never could refuse.

    Oh, what a hero's life could be,
        You see,
    For if I were a hero, if I were a hero.
        If I we're a hero you'd be loving me.

The hero could handle danger,
help any wayward stranger,
Face any obstacle
and never turn away.

His woman, he'd always treasure,
knew how to give her pleasure,
The kind of lovin'
she prayed for everyday.

Oh what a hero's life could be,
You see,
For if I were a hero,
You'd be loving me.

Oh what a hero's life could be,
You see,
For if I were a hero, if I were a hero.
If I we're a hero you'd be loving me.

Love Says Goodbye

You want to go —
Well, I won't even try to hold you back,
Yeah, that's a fact.
I realize that lately you've seemed
Oh so troubled.
Yeah, I can tell the signs,
And though you swear your love for me is gone,
I'll keep on keeping on —
With all we planned,
I understand
That it's not you, but Love who says goodbye.

How many know,
Just how many know that Love is real?
It's more than what you feel.
We come alive in its presence,
And sometimes baby
It's the party who decides
That it no longer wants to be around,
We ran it in the ground.
So dry your eyes
And realized
That it's not you, but Love who says goodbye.

Love says goodbye,
Love says goodbye,
Love says goodbye,
Love says goodbye,

Sure I feel the pain,
But I know Love will come again.
For I know, I know, I know
It will find it's way to me.

You want to go —
Well, I won't even try to hold you back,
Yeah, that's a fact.
I realize that lately you've seemed
Oh so troubled.
Yeah, I can tell the signs
And though you swear your love for me is gone,
I'll keep on keeping on —
With all we planned,
I understand
That it's not you, but Love who says goodbye.

Love says goodbye,
Love says goodbye,
Love says goodbye,
Love says goodbye,

You've Got Something Real

It's not the road we travel on,
It's not the things we say.
It's how we live that makes us strong,
And you have shown me the way,
Shown the way.

It's not how much we give or take,
It's not how far we go.
It's hand-in-hand through each mistake
That helps to make us grow,
Don't you know.

Chorus:
Yeah, you've got, you've got,
You've got something real,
Yeah, you've got, you've got,
You've got something real.

It's not the search for lasting love.
It's not the price we pay.
It's living it, I'm talking of.
You live your love each day,
In every way.

It's not the throne we sit upon.
It's not the cross we bear.
It's taking time to touch someone,
And let them know you care,
You're always there.

Chorus:

Bridge:
So many others lead separate lives,
Facing their own fears everyday.
To afraid to sacrifice,
To take a chance or take it twice.
Just afraid.

(Repeat 1st and 2nd verses and chorus to end.)

Just Lovin' You for a Lifetime

It's hard for me to see
Love lasting forever dear.
It's hard for me to understand
Just how love can last that long.

But what I do believe,
Love is like the gentle wind,
And warms the heart like the sun.
Yes, my love for you is strong.

We don't need to walk
Hand in hand through eternity.
As long as you're by my side
As we go from day to day.

Other people talk,
Swearin' love for evermore,
But the moment the heartaches come,
They're the first to walk away.

Chorus:
Just lovin' you for a lifetime.
Lovin' you for now
Is all I ever want babe,
That we should grow somehow
I won't promise you forever,
For forever is far too long
Just to love you for a lifetime
Is all I ever want.

It's hard for me to see
Love lasting forever dear.
It's hard for me to understand
Just how love can last that long.

But what I do believe,
Love is like the gentle wind,
And warms the heart like the sun.
Yes my love for you is strong.

(Chorus to end.)

What You Gonna Do for Me?

Turn off the lights,
I've seen the sights.
    I'm not impressed by you.
Yeah, take 'em down
Cause I've been around,
    I've seen the work you do.

    Chorus I:
    There are voices raised in misery,
    There are dreams fading from sea to empty sea,
    So much potential wasted in hypocrisy.
    What you gonna do for me?

Like merry-go-rounds
With ups and downs
    And fortune's gone in a glance.
Just end the ride.
Come on inside,
    See how the rest of us dance.

    Chorus II:
    There are voices raised for liberty,
    So much confusion as far as I can see.
    Selling lies, where's your integrity
    Yeah, what you gonna do for me?

I'm Praying for One Tonight

Just one gentle hand to hold,
Is something that I pray for
    Each night,
Waiting for the morning.

But love is hard to find I'm told,
So many never sharing,
Never even caring.

    Chorus:
    But I, I believe there are those
    Who feel love deep inside --
    An I'm praying for one tonight.

Just to share another's life,
Is something that I yearn for
    Each day.
I know it's coming my way.

Others say, "Don't waste your time,
For love has lost its meaning.
Everyone is scheming, (chorus)

  Bridge:
  Someone who's for real.
  Someone who is true.
  Someone who gives their love
    Like I give too.

(Repeat 1st verse and chorus, repeat and fade.)

Shoot for the Sky

The money was out of sight,
I played the game through most of the night,
Thinking my returns were incomplete.
My weaknesses were their device,
I raised the ante, rolled the dice --
Leaving me no corner for retreat.

Chorus:
Might as well shoot for the sky,
Shoot for the sky-y-y-y-y-
I can only hit a cloud.

The woman was so divine,
She looked so good, 'twould be a crime
If I didn't try to play the game.
I took a breath and moved at last,
The line I gave her could shatter glass,
I told her that "Good Lovin'" was my name.

Chorus:

Bridge:
I ain't got nothin' to lose by tryin' what I do.
And when it works out fine it makes a dream come true.

I used to be terrified,
I never looked, I never tried.
I laid the rules with easy passing grades.
Bur there is no good reason why,
We should sit at home, self-satisfied,
Thinking we're ahead of life's parade. (Chorus)

Stroke for Stroke
(Written with Keith Gonzales)

Chorus:
Stroke for stroke, stroke for stroke,
Stroke for stroke, stroke for stroke.

I'm tasting salty water,
It's comin' over me.
Tryin' to keep my balance --
A swimmin' in your sea.

Strokin' to the rhythm,
Waves against my chest.
Soakin' up your lovin'
Can hardly catch my breath. (Chorus)

Bridge:
Strokin' to the rhythm.
The pressure is building, it's just too great,
My body starts to tingle,
The fellin' is pounding, it just can't wait.

Break
Got to get to you,
Look out I'm comin' through
Stroke, stroke, stroke, stroke,
Stroke, stroke, stroke, strooooke -- (chorus)

Repeat 2nd verse.

My heart is really pumpin'
My blood is running sky-i-high.
A tidal wave is comin'
It's gonna blow you mind. (Chorus, then break to end.)

One-Way Love

You know she takes all that he can give her,
And she waits knowing he'll deliver
All her dreams on a silver platter.

Knowing that he'd give his all for a taste of her love.
    One-way love.
Knowing that all he could give was never enough.
    One-way love.

On her face there are mystic traces
Of a young embrace lost in shallow places.
In her heart nothing ever matters.

Love is a street and she is ahead of the game.
    One-way love.
Keep it one way and one never will feel any pain.

    Chorus:
    One-way love, one-way love.
    One-way love, one-way love.
    One-way love, one-way love.
    One-way love, one-way love.

Yeah, she's cool, like an undertaker.
She knows the rules, no man will ever take her.
In her eyes there's a silent laughter.

Many a lover left crying when she went away.
She never cried, she had managed to keep it one way.

(Chorus)

If she cries, it will be tomorrow
For she can't hide all the pain and sorrow,
And in time soon the ice will shatter.

Walls will fall in while she's there standing alone.
    One-way love.
All of those years without love will turn her to stone.
    One-way love.

(Chorus, repeat to end.)

A Kwanzaa Song

On winter's day, past solstice end,
We join with mind and heart again.
Our spirits move to be as one,
Oh, the time for Kwanzaa has begun,

Ancestors know our heart's desire,
We yearn to light the sacred fire.
For seven day we share a truth
And pass our love on to our youth.

Chorus:
Kwanzaa, time of giving,
Kwanzaa time of living,
A time to shine.
And share with all mankind
The true meaning of Kwanzaa

Umoja is to be as one,
And live as children of the sun.
Kujichagulia is to know the way,
No matter what the others say.

To work as one is Ujima
As once we did in Africa,
Ujamma is to share the wealth,
For sharing is to love yourself.

Chorus:

Give purpose to what you do each day,
For Nia helps to find the way.
Kuumba is to let it flow
And create a world where we can grow.

Imani means, "I know we can."
So, spread the faith throughout the land.
No matter what, we rise above,
Cause Kwanzaa's always filled with love.

(Chorus - twice to end.)

Song Lyrics From 1991 to 2000

Good Love, A Healing Pain

Here's a story of love and pain.
Of a man beaten down,
    Till he didn't know his name.
One too many hits, just too many scars.
The woman was a beauty,
    But she had gone too far.

Dirt was treated better, slime was lookin' good.
What he saw in this woman,
    No one understood.
Some are lead by the nose, some are lead by the neck.
When all was said and done,
    He was quite a wreck.

Chorus:
But he'd be smilin'
Like a man in sane.
Mumbling something,
"Good love, good love is a healing pain!"
He was whipped into a corner.
Heart bond and chained.
Still swearing,
"Good love, good love is a healing pain!"

(Repeat verses and chorus.)

Crossroad†

Obstacles planted long ago
　　Have all begun to bloom,
Life's in winter's bitter cold,
　　Beneath a veil of doom.
For time has turned it's face away,
　　As younger dreams move on their way;
As I sit here at this crossroad in my life.

Undecided where to go,
　　I feel I've lost my way.
I thought I knew it year ago
　　Before I learned to stray,
And now I search for old road signs,
　　The kind I read when youth was mine;
As I sit here at this crossroad in my life.

　　Chorus I:
　　Left, right, hold tight
　　　　Maybe it's straight ahead.
　　I'm lost, coin toss.
　　　　It's choices that I dread.
　　For fear has hindered my desire,
　　　　With failure cooling down the fire
　　As I sit here, in my niche here,
　　　　From this ditch here, it's a bitch here
　　　　　　At I this crossroad in my life.

Lead

As I sit here at this crossroad in my life

Obstacles planted long ago
Have all begun to bloom,
Life's in winter's bitter cold,
Beneath a veil of doom.
For time has turned it's face away
As younger dreams move on their way;
As I sit here at this crossroad in my life.

Chorus II:
Left, right, hold tight
Maybe it's straight ahead
I'm lost, coin toss,
It's choices that I dread.
For fear has hindered my desire,
With failures cooling down the fire
As I sit here, in my niche here,
It's a bitch here, but I won't quit here,
At I this crossroad in my life.

When You Play with Fire†

Children raising children who walk the line of fate,
Some are born in a house of love, others born in hate.
Sure they need direction, but daddy's on the run.
Soon to feel a nation bleed from a man-child with a gun.

When you play with fire, something's gotta,
Something's gotta burn.
When you play with fire, something, somewhere,
Some how's gotta burn.

Teacher's preach semantics, proper nouns and verbs.
Children stare with vacant eyes, no one's heard a word;
Because they're plagued by questions, too few dare to breach
Like please divide the Art of War into the number of number of the Beast.

When you play with fire, something's gotta,
Something's gotta burn.
When you play with fire, something, somewhere,
Some how's gotta burn.

Quick to list solutions, slow to find the cause.
No one sees the monsters in the mirror down the hall.
No one spots the lightning, no one hears the screams;
Desolation's time for glory, tell me what it means.

When you play with fire, something's gotta,
Something's gotta burn.
When you play with fire, something, somewhere,
Some how's gotta burn.

Soldiers on the ready, missiles on the rise.
Nations are capitulating, the body count is high.
Children caught in the middle, get a window with a view.
While up on high the Dogs of War are waiting for their cue.

When you play with fire, something's gotta,
Something's gotta burn.
When you play with fire, something, somewhere,
Some how's gotta burn.
Gotta burn, (Repeat and fade.)

Another Child Is Gone

Children in the age of innocence,
Smothered by a silent crime.
Rapture in the guise of ignorance,
Reveals itself in time.
As children of the Spirit,
Abused within the lust,
Battered in each cycle,
Surrender up, surrender up,
Surrender up, surrender up
    Their trust.

    Chorus:
    Don't you even tarry,
    Don't you weep too long,
    Before this song is over,
    Another child is gone.

Tomorrow lies in stillness,
In shadows stark and bold,
As children become the victims
Their stories dark and cold.
When love-ones become the strangers,
Who rule with back of hand,
And sugar plums and dreams that come
Lie broken, lie broken,
Lie broken, lie broken
    Where they stand.

    Chorus

Bridge:
Who do they listen to
    When truth becomes a lie?
Tell me, can they reach out to you
Or would you rather, rather see them die.

    Chorus to bridge.

Ain't No Blues*†

Strife woke me up one morning,
    It said, "Son, how goes your day?
Is there any grief I can bring you
    Or pain to throw you way?"

I said, "There's nothing you got
    Can touch me.
No hurtin' so bad, you can ever send,
    For Ain't no blues,
        Ain't no blues,
        Ain't no blues like losin' a friend."

Well, hardship tried to overcome me,
    It said, "I can make you feel like all is in vain.
And put all odds against you,
    Though you try and try again."

I said, "Well, when life comes round
    Full circle,
You can put all your hardships end to end,
    But Ain't no blues,
        Ain't no blues,
        Ain't no blues like losin' a friend. (Repeat last 3 lines.)

Bridge:
When I needed to talk,
    You were there to walk me home.
Yeah, I know you still care,
    Cause I know that you're there.
        Still it hurts being alone.

Strife woke me up one morning,
It said, "Son, how goes your day?
Is there any grief I can bring you.
Or pain to throw you way?"

I said, "There's nothing you got
Can touch me.
No hurtin' so bad, you can ever send,
For Ain't no blues,
Ain't no blues,
Ain't no blues like losin' a friend."
Ain't no blues,
Ain't no blues,
Ain't no blues, no blues, no blues,
Ain't no blues like losin' a friend."

*Written while riding on the subway to work. Thinking about the sudden passing of my childhood friend, my best friend Donn Lowe, the day before, who died unexpectedly of a heart attack on May 18th, 1998. Sung by Keith Gonzales (another close friend) and myself at his funeral. Donn and I grew up together, met in elementary school, and started playing music together in the early sixties..

Neath the City Lights†

Neath the city lights, countless souls abide.
Some in agony, some too proud to cry.
Some are reaching out with a yearning in their heart,
Pleading for a meaning to their lives.
I am one of them,
Neath the city lights.

Neath these walls of stone, love is hard to find.
Many walk alone, so all along – shadows lost in time.
Through their weeping eyes, they're calling to someone,
"Hold me, love me with all your might!"
Are you one of them?
Neath the city lights.

We've seen their faces in the mirror of
Broken dreams.
Hiding the traces of their pain and misery –
Oh, so quietly
Neath the city lights.

On these crowded streets strangers crossing paths.
It's our chance to meet, hoping something lasts.
With a fearful glance we open up our hearts,
Revealing all the need within our lives.
Won't you talk with me?
Won't you walk with me?
Maybe share love with me,
Neath the city lights.

Then I See You†

Hands are shaky, nerve endings fried.
Caring so much tears me up inside.
Feeling elated, like kissing the breeze,
But "answers to questions" is what I need.

Chorus:
Oh like, am I in love or am I in pain?
Can't tell the difference, it seems all the same.
For if I'm in love, tell me, what did I gain?
Then I see you. (Oh, I see you – for 2nd and last chorus)

Sleepless tomorrows, yet I just can't complain.
I tremble like thunder before the rain.
Anxiously waiting, trying to cope
With changes upon changes, still I need to know. (Chorus)

Bridge:
Heartache. Pleasure. It's harder than ever to read the signs.
Go on. No please stay. Why can't I make up my mind?

(Repeat 1st verse, and then repeat chorus twice to ending.)

Stand Up, Stand Down†

Some people take things for granted,
 Some people take cause they'll never receive,
Some people take without asking,
 When the bottom line is — just take what you need.

Some people give for no reason,
 Some people give, yet they'll never receive.
Some people give without asking,
 Takes a special kind to fulfill a need.

 Chorus I:
 Who am I to spend my life awake,
 Wondering who is giving or who takes.
 I can hear voices saying, "Catch me if you can."
 Who's holding your baby's hand,
  Don't you understand — or is it too late?

Some people fight with compassion.
 Some people fight at the drop of a dime,
Some people fight without asking
 Where their orders come from — in truth that's the crime.

Some people love without question,
 Some people love, cause they think it's sublime.
Some people love understanding
 It's the only gift to offer mankind.

Chorus II:
Who am I to live my life in fright,
Wondering who is loving or who fights.
I can hear voices saying, "Catch me if you can."
Invading the promise land,
    Don't you understand — or is it too late?

Main Chorus:
Stand up, stand down.
What goes around comes around,
Stand up, stand down.
What goes around still comes around.
Stand up, stand down .....
Stand up, stand down,
What goes around, still comes around

(Repeat verses 1, 2, and chorus I -- main chorus and chorus 2)

Lady on a Train

Faces locked in anger
    That echoes along the rail,
There's a screech and doors slide open
    To the sadness that prevails.
As heroes draped in failure
    File in this cattle car.
And in this sea of vacant eyes,
    I glimpse a shining star.

In this press-the-flesh compartment,
    Where our hopes hang out to dry.
And the heads bob to the rhythm
    It's hard to catch her eye.
A queen in copper beauty,
    As splendid as the Nile.
And if God still rides this subway,
    I need to see you smile.

Chorus:
It's crazy to ponder,
But I'd give praises to his name.
To feel your smile go through me
    (Alt: Cause I know your smile could heal me)
As I ride this subway train.

This iron horse is crazy,
    It tends to bend the mind.
It dims your dreams to hazy
    And leaves them far behind.
But now and then pure heaven,
    Will pass on through those doors,
And in their eyes, a fire
    To make your spirit soar.

(Repeat chorus to end.)

Broken Glass†

Down on the corner in ragged clothes.
Where she stays nobody knows.
She makes a scene from time to time,
Deep in her cups and talking wine.
Tattered in the heart,
Shattered like broken glass.

She was a looker in '44
They sent her fly boy off to war.
Shot down his plane, blew up her life,
Her burnin' dreams turned cold as ice.
Tattered in the heart,
Shattered like broken glass.

You hear her cryin', "Ain't love supposed to last?"

They had a son she tried to raise
Through lonely years of empty days.
She swore the drink could set her right,
And keep her warm on winter nights.
Tattered in the heart,
Shattered like broken glass.

They say the child just ran away,
Tired of the pain he had to pay.
She took to livin' on the streets,
Lookin' for a love she couldn't keep.
Tattered in the heart,
Shattered like broken glass.

You hear her cryin', "Ain't love supposed to last?"

Bridge:
How thin the line we walk along the ledge,
For most of us still teeter on the edge,
And when we fall, we fall oh, so fast,
And when we hit – broken glass.

Down on the corner in ragged clothes,
Where she stays nobody knows.
Some say she's mean, some say she's kind,
Most say she's lost her peace of mind.
Tattered in the heart,
Shattered like broken glass.

The moral lies within her eyes,
Between the tears and heavy sighs.
Though you may come, don't come this way.
Find the strength to face another day
Tattered in the heart,
Shattered like broken glass.

You hear her cryin'...

Workin' to Be Poort

Workin' hard from dusk till dawn.
Flesh is weak, spirit worn.
Bags of bottles by the tens,
Multiply by five cents.

At every corner he takes a pause,
Inspects the goods, discards the flaws.
He wheels his load with special care.
This tattered man, we watch and stare.

I am amazed.
I swear, what's it all for?
He's working harder every day, Lord.
Just workin', workin', workin'
Workin' to be poor

In heat, in cold, in driving rain,
Sets to his task, conceals his pain.
And there's no way to empathize
Or heal the look deep in his eyes.

Society demands the best.
Some win, some lose, some more or less,
But until we've walked his hallowed ground,
We best not even make a sound.

I am amazed.
I swear, what's it all for?
He's working harder every day, Lord.
Just workin', workin', workin'
Workin' to be poor

And as he goes I seize the chance
To contemplate my circumstance.
As debtors come and debtors go;
One step ahead of being broke.

Some thirty years of nine to fives,
The dreams still come, few stay alive.
And for all my pain, it makes no sense,
Coming out ahead by five cents.

I am amazed.
I swear, what's it all for?
I'm working harder every day, Lord.
Just workin', workin', workin'
Workin' to be poor (repeat this line 4x)

Genocide†

Brother, have you lost your mind,
Dreaming of a promise land so very few will find?
Hanging, swaying in the trees.
Bodies that look a lot like me.
Daddy says, "Son, close your eyes so you won't see
The genocide."

Mama, deep within your prayer.
Speakin' to your only son, they took when you weren't there.
Prisons with death in every cage.
Choke holds, an answer to their rage.
Daddy says, "Shit! We're deep within the age
Of genocide."

It matters not the time or season,
Hatred doesn't need a reason
To fill the world with pain.
Slaughter comes with cold indifference,
Marching on the path of least resistance.
Are we all to blame?

Children, children of the sun,
Trading in your destiny for a six pack or a gun.
Ah, bullets, the stories they could tell.
Drive-bys, how many can you kill?
Daddy says, "Son, you must be above the swell
Of genocide.

"Someone give me water, someone give me air!"
Cries the lofty preacher, "Heavenly Father are you there?
Give us shelter from the storm.
Lead us to where we can do no wrong."
Daddy says, "Son, don't let this be the norm.
    This genocide."

  Is it the fault of being human,
  That some of us will seek to cause confusion
  Through the taste of blood?
  While genocide controls its minions,
  Cutting short the life of countless millions. . . .
  Where the hell is Love?

People, open up your minds.
    Listen to the Inner Voice, we need so much to find.
Spirits are calling from the grave,
    "Mankind, when will you come of age?"
Daddy says, "What is there left to save
    From genocide?

Can we stop the genocide?
Help me stop the genocide.

One Can Never Tell†

Days on concrete, years on a dusty road,
The choice of freedom is hard.
Strife in the city, frustration overload,
Too many secrets of the heart.

Once called a treasure, now just a son of a bitch,
Far from the apple of their eye.
Looking for shelter, still trying to fill that niche,
In some deep, dark corner of the pie.

Chorus:
And there's no way
You're ever going back to that persecution.
No way in hell.
Maybe some day,
You'll reach a point of resolution. Who knows?
One can never tell.

Truth is a monster, better to live a lie.
Visions you held are all but gone.
Acting the hustler, pimping up alibis.
One puff, one scam and you belong.

Family behind you, echoes of yesterday.
No one knows where the hell you are.
Runaway fever, pushing you far away
From all those secrets of the heart.

Chorus:

Break:

Space is a vacuum, your mind just a cluttered mess,
Time is a place to feel your pain.
Youth is a passion, Life the ultimate test,
Without a lost, there is no gain.

Child of the cycle, babe of the lullaby,
Who was the one who crushed your heart?
Love filled with terror, they don't even realize
How much they tear a life apart.

Chorus:

Is Anybody Out There?

Is anybody out there?
Can anybody see?
I'm movin' through some hard times,
Blind as blind as blind can be.
Some say there's a reason,
Some say it's just because.
I've yet to see he daylight, daylight,
Lordy, lord, lord, lord.

Is anybody listening?
Can anybody hear?
The screamin's gettin' louder, louder.
It's worse than what I feared.
They say that it's a season.
Some say it's just a phase.
I'm shattered by the silence, silence
Growing, growing day by day.

Chorus:
I'm down on my knees praying,
Just like a child in fear.
Lord, you know I'm aching,
Make this pain disappear, disappear

Bridge:
Lord hold me in you gentle arms,
Help me to rise above.
Keep me safe from harm,
Show me your sacred love.
Touch me with a healing hand
Someday I might understand
What's it all for, what's it all for.

Is anybody coming?
Does anybody care?
This load is getting heavy, so heavy.
Please, someone say a prayer.
They say there is a Oneness,
Some swear it ain't so.
I just need a hand to guide me,
In this darkness here below.

Chorus to end.

Your Eyes†

You eyes reveal so much than you do.
They capture the essence of you
For all the world to see.

Like stars with secrets of love to unfold,
And when the story is told,
You'll be lovin' me.

Chorus:
Shimmer, glitter,
Warm and tender windows of your soul
Pools of passion,
Can't imagine love turning cold
In your eyes.

My heart surrendered with one single glance.
Your eyes never gave it a chance.
I'm forever yours.

In time, when other loves fade in the night.
Ours will burning bright.
Of this I know for sure.

Chorus:

(Repeat 1st verse and chorus, ending with "In your eyes" 3x.)

Drinkin' the Blues‡

Walkin' home in the rain,
Bleeding heartache, oozing pain.
Feelin' like you've died,
Cause nothin's left inside
After drinkin' the blues.

Mornin' coffee, all alone.
That damn one note on the telephone.
Seems like every door is closed,
Whenever someone knows
You've been drinkin' the blues

Bridge:
A tall frosted glass of sadness
Is enough to bring you down.
One little sip of gladness
Could turn my life around.

Supper's burnin', yet dinner's cold.
Lord, this boozin' is taking its toll.
Still if anybody cares
I've got a glass to spare,
And we could go drinkin,
We could be drinkin,
We could go drinkin the blues.

Serenade

Serenade the prophet
Sitting on a hill.
Listen to the sermon
And all that is revealed.

For tomorrow there'll be questions
And tests to finalize.

For words can feed a hunger
Like manna on the plain.
They stir an inner thunder
With sounds of heavy rain.
Serenade.

Pay homage to the woman
Who bears a child of truth.
Who feeds the world with wisdom,
Just to perish in their youth.

For one sage is far too many
In a world that's pressed for time.

In a age of wonder,
Still days are dark and cold.
A Prophet stirs the people
And brings them to the fold (with truths never told)
(Oh) serenade

In every life a vision,
We break and then (re)condition.
In every heart an answer,
We just have to let it out.

Serenade the prophet,
Give praises in a song.
Gaze beyond reflections,
And you'll know where you belong.

Let your light shine within you,
Just be and let it out.

The world is lost in questions,
You hold the answers to.
In the mirror of reflection,
The prophet stares at you.
(Oh) serenade

Heart of Gold

From the dim light of a bedroom
Sits a face in darkened tones
Stealing glances at a mirror,
Through his eyes, he watched alone.
Yeah, the years had crept up on him
Since his youth had taken flight.
And time ticked down his chances,
Leaving few to set things right.

There was a wife he rarely cherished,
A son he never met.
There's a daughter with a hunger
And a life full of regrets.
There were years he spent in hiding,
In the garden of the truth,
And as life begins to whither,
He must answer for his youth.

Chorus I:
What are you lookin' at?
How could I have known,
The years spent pushing love away
Would turn my heart to stone?
I don't care if no one loves me,
So what if I'm growing old!
It's too late to light the fire
And turn this heart to gold.

He removed himself from laughter
To avoid a world of grief.
Seeking comfort in the shadows
To support his disbelief.
He gathered strength in loneliness,
He swore he'd never change.
He took pride in his survival,
In his shackles, and his chains.

He saw his life a labor,
His labor, he saw a pain.
Refusing to pay life's wages,
Hoarding all that he had gained.
No answers, there were no questions,
No tally at the bottom line.
Just an image in a mirror,
Just a waste of precious time.

> Chorus II:
> Then the bedroom door swung open
> And a grandchild stood inside,
> Saying, "Grandpa, what's the matter?
> Why the sadness in your eyes?
> Why sit here in the darkness?
> Won't you come into the light?
> Let me put my arms around you,
> Let me hug you, oh so tight.

Heart of Gold (Cont'd)

The child's words weighed upon (on) him
As the spirit touched his heart,
And the stone began to soften
In the fire, from the spark.
And a shiver ran right through him,
From a yearning deep inside.
And as this child held him tenderly,
The tears flowed from his eyes.

Chorus III:
No sense in lookin' back,
How could he have been wrong?
A need buried so deep within
Was rising all along.
It brought him sweet surrender
And peace or so I'm told.
And in the little time remaining,
He found a heart of gold.

I Should've Seen It Coming

Toward the bedroom walking
Leaving a trail of crumbs.
Her eyes enticed my senses
"Well son, do you want some?"

My feet moved to the notion,
My heart jumped at the chance.
Like a horse drawn to water,
I followed in a trance.

Chorus:
I should've seen it coming,
I should've let it lay.
For a book up on her mantle read,
"How to skin your prey."

But addition wasn't my strong suit,
It's much better to multiply.
One times one equals lots of fun
To a younger man's eyes.

One pamphlet read, Snuff and Stuff,
Another read, Lunch and Munch.
The sign above here bedpost read,
They Only Come Here Once!

(Chorus)

You Must Believe

Searching through the heavens
For an astral sign,
Looking for a miracle
That would free his mind.
Praying in the temples,
All these many years,
Stands in discuss,
Damn, no one hears.

A soldier in remission,
Far from the battle cry,
Longing for an answer,
At least a reason why.
Cannot hide the guilt
Can't wash away the stain.
Early one morning,
A voice spoke through his pain.

It said, "You must believe
Beyond your faith.
You must believe,
Whatever it takes.
It may be hard, son.
No matter what, the spirit's One.

Woke in a fever,
    Thought he lost his mind.
Never had a vision,
    None of any kind.
Finished his drink
    Crawled back to bed.
But there written on the wall
    The fateful words that read.

No need for mass confusion,
    Let it melt into the sun.
Life and death are back to back,
    The dance has just begun.
And chaos pleads surrender,
    When weary of the game.
As order sings one note, one song
    And whispers one sweet name.

For every lost illusion
    Will draw into the whole.
And paint a clearer picture
    //: One spirit, one love, one soul.:// (Repeat and fade.)

Thought You Were All Alone

Who's been digging through your dirt?
Going through you garbage
Finding stuff you thought well hid?

Sifting with a fine comb?
Post-its from you pocket.
Surveillance in the place where you live.

Chorus:
And you thought you were all alone,
So insignificant,
You wouldn't hurt a fly,
Well, so did, so did, so did, so did I.

Who's been shadowing your shadow?
Downloading your passwords.
Identity's a thing we all share.

Skeletons in the closet,
Dining with a stranger,
Resurrecting every sin you can spare.

Chorus;;

Bridge:
Take a memo to my doctor,
A letter to my priest,
Tell all my confidants, I'll be out of reach.
Take my baby pics and shred them,
Set my diaries up in flames.
Tell someone at the courthouse
To please erase my name,
Till nothing else remains.

You've been searching for that island,
Scouring for that cave,
A place to runaway from it all.

But wherever you go,
They got you by the numbers
Others got you by (yeah, them too).

Chorus to end.

In My Darkest Hour

In the marrow of my anguish
The darkness hid my light.
Where every turn
Was just one more turn astray

I had no better friend than sorrow.
Lord, how grief could set things right.
I didn't know better,
Just lost along the way.

One thousand and one sad reasons
Why life treats me so bad.
For I felt that no one
Could heal me anyway.

Just to wallow in my sadness
Till the pain would drive me mad.
Destroyin' myself
Was how I spent my day

Chorus;;
And in my darkest hour
You found me.
And in my greatest need you came.
You put your loving arms around me
Till my tears fell down like rain.
Please hold me, hold me.
Till my sun shines again.

Oh, the time I wasted
Nurturing the hurt inside.
It's time I felt, time I felt
The love I had denied. (Chorus, 1st verse to chorus)

Premonition

I got a premonition
    Someone's gonna burn tonight.
Just from her expression,
    Pull the shades, dim the lights.
Hey, man, I'd pack myself a suitcase.

    Chorus:
    She's smokin' in the corner,
    Daggers shooting from her red eyes.

I could swear that look's familiar.
    Yeah, I've seen it once in flight.
I had a buddy who saw it also.
    The night his lady shot him twice.

    Chorus:

  Bridge:
  Man, I'd leave that woman alone.
  That look could turn a man to stone.

(First verse and chorus to end.)

Where We Coming From?

It's four in the morning, where you from?
I see it in your eyes, but you're far too young.
Who taught you how to sell?
Who taught you how to feed?
Is there nothin' left that's sacred,
    Nothin' but the need?
And she walked off into the night,
Yelling, "Hey, man, where you coming from?"
And she walked off into the night,
Yelling, "Hey, man, where you coming from?"

Sitting on a doorstep counting every scar.
Each track and rainbow that took him too far.
Somebody's mother's child,
Someone who had dreams.
Now nothing but the nightmares,
Come and make him scream.
And as he nods off into the night,
I wonder, "Where we coming from?"
As he nods off into the night,
I wonder, "Where we coming from?"

Bridge:
The road to the future
Leads through the past.
And if we keep going round and round,
How much longer will it last?

Lead

And as he nods off into the night,
I wonder, "Where we coming from?"

Huddled 'neath cardboard, 'gainst the freezing cold.
Faces all too young, some far too old.
Where do we draw the line,
Stop the waste and greed?
And live by the simple phrase,
"Love is all you need."
And as I walk off into the night,
I wonder, "Where we coming from?"
As I walk off into the night,
I wonder, "Where we coming from?"
As I walk off into the night, I wonder.

Not for Sale

My heart it not for sale,
    Your plans, babe, will only fail.
My heart is dedicated to just one love.
Don't even think you can
    Trip me up, pull me down with that stuff.

You swear, babe, your love is real.
    All I know is what I feel.
Don't want to play these silly games anymore.
Do me one favor,
    Stay away, out of sight of my door.

    Chorus:
    I've got to stay the course,
    Keep my eyes wide open now.
    Watch 'round every corner,
    There are women on the prowl.
    Hold myself together,
    Keep my mind in check.
    Sex is circling up above
    There are women on the deck.
    One false move and,
    Sure enough, one winds up in some bed.

You whisper so many lies
    While flirting those sultry eyes.
Hoping to slide your ice-cold frigid hands into mine.
Turn off the juices,
    Douse the flame, hold the soup, cork the wine.

Decisions

Made a choice, some regrets,
Gave up love and cigarettes.
Still, I'm okay, a little blue,
    But color is only a hue.

Mama says I must decide,
Stay at home or live outside,
Now that's a drag, at least it seems
    Sometimes life can be so, so mean.

    Chorus:
    Too many decisions,
        What am I suppose to do?
    Too many decisions,
        What is my world coming to?
    When I try to decide,
        I would much rather hide,
    Cause I haven't got a clue.
    Oh, too many decisions
        Is gonna break this brain in two.

All my friends have gone coed.
What's with him? I heard it said.
Make up your mind, sometime today
    So tired of the games we play.

Every day I've gotta chose,
Ante up, then win or lose.
There's no escape, no reprieve,
    There's something better, I gotta believe.

    Chorus:

Why So Many Holes in the Road?

Mind if I take a seat?
I mean like, can we just talk awhile?
I could sure use the company,
Cause today's been a real ball-buster chile.

I'm just tryin' to make ends meet.
With one end north, the other south,
And no cash in between,
Yeah, I can see you know what I'm talkin' about.

It's not easy to walk the walk,
No written guarantee.
So many talk the talk,
So very few every succeed.

Like a bird I try to fly,
But I keep crashing, crashing to the ground.
People say, "Son it's 'bout your time rise."
But, whenever I look up, all I see is down.

Chorus:
And nobody, nobody seems to know,
Why there so many holes in the road.
And I've got to carry this crazy load
With so many, so many holes in the road.

Would you like another drink?
Hey, bar keep, slice us another round.
Come on now, tell me what you think,
Should I stay or get the hell outta town?

Yeah, I thought about makin' tracks,
But then I thought about payin' dues.
And after I viewed all the facts,
I figured it's time I learn to play the blues.

Lead -- Chorus:

Well, I guess it's time fore me to go,
Lord knows, I've wasted enough of your time.
You know, life can beat you down with a rubber hose,
And they don't even call it a crime (ouch).

Yeah, well you just watch your step out there,
All footloose and fancy free,
Happy- go-lucky without a care,
Chile, there's always one hole you won't see.

Chorus to end, repeat "ahh, so many," end with "holes in the road."

Lovin' You for Real

I tried lovin' you sober,
Tried lovin' you blind.
I've tried a million ways baby,
    Failed each and every time.
I'm at my wits end.
Hell, I'm gonna go with what I feel.
This time I'm gonna love ya,
    Love you for real.

I've tried lovin' you rich, babe,
Tried lovin' you poor,
I'd put my life on mortgage,
    Just don't walk out that door.
I'd be lost without you,
A pain too hard to conceal (ah, baby)
This time I'm gonna love ya,
    Love you for real.

Bridge:
I thought I could play the field,
Still swearin' our love was real,
But I was only foolin' my heart.
Cause baby, you knew the score
And the more I tried to love you more.
The lies would only keep us apart.

(1st verse, repeating last phrase, starting with "This time . . .")

Is It True That You're Leaving?

Is it true that you're leaving
 Just to find some peace of mind?
Take it from me chile,
 You can't leave pain behind.
It's part of the luggage,
 The hardest to unload.
Thought you should know, chile, before you go.

No, life isn't easy,
 Nobody said it was.
Most of our misery
 Comes from those we love.
So wherever you wander,
 Wherever you may roam.
Whenever you need, chile, just come on home.

Bridge:
Don't dwell on the sadness.
Go find you some gladness
 In this game called life.
And for every tomorrow,
 There's alway a sorrow.
Yet, somehow love makes it right.

So, if it's true that you're leaving
 Just to find some peace of mind.
Take it from me, chile,
 You can't leave pain behind.
It travels on with you,
 And touches every need.
Thought you should know, chile, before you leave.

Riding This White Horse

Stuck in this shadow,
Trapped in this frame of a body, Lord.
Stirred into madness.
Crazy is a mind I can afford.

Words tied together
Into knots that hold me down.
Strapped in this saddle
Riding this white horse,
    Riding this white horse,
        Riding this white horse into the ground.

A flicker of childhood
With signs on every wall.
From taboos to totems,
The holes were there for me to fall.

But I stormed the castle,
The hero who was a clown,
Now I'm strapped in this saddle
Riding this white horse,
    Riding this white horse,
        Riding this white horse into the ground.

Bridge:
And all the forms that pass me by,
Shake their heads and wonder why,
So much potential, so much potential.
I dip and nod and drool the rest,
This stupor makes me look grotesque
Cause I'm strapped in this saddle.

As I ride into darkness,
There are eyes I can't betray.
I am the totem,
I am the sign to stay away.

Some heed the warnings
They're those who mess around.
Soon they'll be strapped in the saddle
Riding this white horse,
Riding this white horse,
Riding this white horse into the ground.

Black Widow

She walked in, the place got cold.
She'll chill your heart, steal your soul.
Lips that could light a fire in any man.
Ooh, what a woman.
    Lord, help me out, the best you can.

    Chorus;
    Black Widow, her claim to fame.
    Just one kiss, no man's the same.
    She circled the room and
        Each man could feel the heat.
    Terror / desire, Lord, what a place
        For them to meet.

  Bridge:
  Just to watch here move,
      Eyes burnin' through you now.
  Got to hold myself together,
      Black Widow's on the prowl.
  Searching for a lover,
      Lookin' for a meal.
  God, that woman's so divine,
      I can't help the way I feel.
  And I'm still shaking,
      It's a feelin' I can't conceal.

Lead and chorus

She sees me, there's no escape.
Caught in her web, I took the bait.
Every move she weaves, says, "You're mine."
Yes, I surrender, just be gentle, just be kind.

Bridge II:
Just to watch her move,
  Eyes burnin' through you now.
Couldn't hold myself together
  With Black Widow on the prowl.
She found herself a lover,
  Found herself a meal.
God, that woman's so divine,
  Can't help the way I feel.
But it's too late,
  Ah, man, what's the big deal.

Come Child (Naming Ceremony)

Come child,
Come before us.
Give us your hand.
Come join in the circle of woman and man.

Come child,
Hear the whisper.
Let us learn you name.
The spirits bless you and let us do the same.

Chorus:
Come child,
Blessed child.
Come child
Beautiful African child.
Come child,
Come to stay.
Come join you people, let us show you the way.

Come child
Taste the future.
Heed us when we call.
We've come to stand
Here beside you and never let you fall.

Come child
Share the wonder,
From daylight through the night
Make sure to gather
Some wisdom and add it to your life.

Chorus, repeat 1st verse and chorus)

Looking for a Place in Your Heart

Someone's in pain tonight,
Feelin' the strain tonight,
Just hurtin' as dreams fall apart.
Someone's in misery,
Then again maybe its only me
Who's watchin' the world from the dark.

Someone is torn tonight
Cause something's gone wrong tonight.
And sorry just won't mend anymore.
Lookin' through a veil of tears,
At the one thing I always feared --
You walking, walking out the door.

Chorus:
For no matter how you justify,
I can't accept the reasons why you had to go,
And I'm anxious for another chance,
Just waiting for the circumstance
To let you know
I'm just lookin' for a place in your heart,
Yeah, I'm just lookin' for a place in your heart.

Someone is lost tonight,
Paying the cost tonight.
Aching for someplace to belong.
Smothered by memories,
And needing some space to breathe.
Just walking the streets till the dawn.

Chorus

(Repeat 1st verse and chorus to end.)

Song Lyrics From 2001 to 2010

Startin' All Over Again‡

Friends say, "Man,
You look like a mess."
Well, I've been better, I must confess.
But I've been through hard times,
Seen hunger, pain.
I've got to start all over again.

Won't blame the women,
Can't blame the work.
No excuses Lord, I'm just a jerk.
Man, I'm so angry,
Still counting to ten.
I've got to start all over again.

Bridge:
I've been through this doggone mill
So many times,
You wouldn't believe me,
But it's nobody else's fault but mine.
Listen to me.

I've been humbled,
Knocked to my knees,
Cut down to size, 180 degrees.
Still, I am grateful
For this chance to begin,
I get to start all over again.

(Repeat bridge and last verse - Startin' All Over Again)

So Glad You Came

Oh, they said you weren't coming,
Just another way for me to lose.
They told me you'd be busy,
With much better things to do.
Now you put them all to shame,
So glad you came.

Heard there was a wager
You know these ears can burn.
With excuses by the dozen
You'd put me down at every turn..
Now you put them all to shame,
So glad you came.

Chorus:
So glad you came,
So glad you came,
So glad you came,
So glad you came,
Now you put them all to shame,
So glad you came.

(Repeat 1st verse and chorus.)

So Many Lies

So many lies,
So many bridges burning.
So little time
To find my way back home.
I won't deny, I feel the fire burning.

Mama says, "Swallow you pride,
    Or stay out there
Get off your high horse,
    Show you care.
Ego will lead you, deceive you
    And leave you all alone."

In so many ways
I set my pain in motion.
I am amazed at the seeds
That I have sown.
In younger days,
I brewed a wicked potion.

Daddy says, "Son, now,
    You've gone too far.
With every relation,
    You leave a scar.
Your hustle for trouble will double,
    And leave you out there in the cold."

Bridge:
Baby, I'm alone out here,
Out here in the cold.
It's taking its toll, dear.
I'm begging, begging to come on home.

(Repeat 1st verse.)

Maybe Somewhere Down the Line

Maybe somewhere down the line,
    There'll be peace to find.
There's a world waiting and bleeding.

I just hope there'll come a day,
    When war's so far away,
We'll say, "Who goes there? Don't know you son."

I'm just one voice in the world,
    So many to be heard,
Each saying, "Don't go there! It's crazy!

Hearts are screamin', "Heed the signs!"
    Don't you lose your mind.
Don't let this world.some crumbling down.

Chorus:
True, I won't try to deny it.
Peace, it's so hard to find it.
Hearts need healing time in Love.

Hate stands ready, down the road,
    With Revenge, I'm told.
Two brothers, both crazy.

They're already spillin' blood,
    Rising to a flood,
In a world stark raving mad.

Chorus:
True, I won't try to deny it.
Peace, it's so hard to find it.
Hearts need healing time in Love.

Surely, somewhere in the dark,
There's a healing spark,
Shining ever so lightly,

Just enough to show the way,
There's no need to stay.
Just remember who we are.

(Chorus and 1st verse to end.)

Got Me Begging

Tell me baby, was it worth it,
To see me down on my knees?
I gave my heart and you hurt it.
Got me begging for you please.
I always thought there was a chance girl,
But you swear all men are the same.
And now it's your chance for revenge, well,
You beat me down, it's a cryin' shame.

Chorus:
Cause I need you, despite the pain.
I know there's lightning,
Still I stand here in the rain.
It wasn't me who broke your heart.
It was another lover,
I'm not that brother.
Just let me love you.

Tell me baby, are you happy
To leave me in misery?
Took my heart and just snapped it,
Saying, "Don't you come crawling back to me."
Yeah, you got me, I surrender.
Never wanted to play this silly game.
If it's what you want, just remember,
You take the loss, you take the blame.

Chorus, break chorus.

Tell me baby, was it worth it,
To see me down on my knees
I gave my hear and you hurt it.
Got me begging for you please.

Too Long in the Rain

Sunlight so far away,
Storms clouds -- here to stay.
Raindrops, like my heart, beat the ground
With every tomorrow tumbling down.

No trace, no beating heart,
Our love -- torn apart.
Sometimes I wonder where, when, or how.
Show me some daylight, I need it now.

Chorus:
(It's been) Too long in the rain,
I can hardly move.
Too long in the rain,
Tell me, what's the use?
Too long in the rain,
Lookin' for reasons why,
Too long in the rain,
Eyes that search on high
In this rain, rain, rain, rain, rain.

Darkness is all around
Gray skies -- still hold me down,
Seasons of heartache -- way too long.
Lord, I know I can beat this -- keep me strong.

Chorus to end.

Pain to Kill‡

Pour me another,
I tell you when to stop.
Nah, that's not enough,
The other shoe hasn't dropped.

Chorus:
I've got pain to kill,
Hear me when I say,
I got pain to kill.
There can be no delay.
I need to numb-ify this heartache,
Gonna drink my belly full,
I got pain to kill.

Hell, just leave the bottle.
Sure I got the cash.
T ain't none of your business.
Aah, man, kiss my ... (Chorus)

Sorry 'bout my manners
Come on let's be friends
Have a drink on me buddy
You know this pain doesn't end (Chorus)

Yeah, there's no denying
I'm only foolin' myself
But for now bear with me son,
And pull one more bottle from that shelf. (Chorus)

Lord knows, it's time to cork it.
Yeah, it's time to quit.
The other shoe has fallen,
And my head's about to split. (Chorus)

Just point me in one direction,
Preferably the door.
Hope I can make it home,
Before I stop(s) and drink some more. (Chorus to end.)

Where Is the Man I Was?

Get me to a doctor,
Feelin' kinda bad.
Queasy with a fever
Teary eyed and sad.
I know we had a quarrel
That grew into a fight.
It doesn't explain the pain I feel tonight.

Get up on your cell phones,
Punch it 9 1 1.
My heart is getting heavy, girl,
Look what you've done.
Thought I was stronger,
Swore I could walk away.
Never felt this before,
Can't explain the hurt I feel today

Chorus 2x
Where is the man I was?
Where is the man I knew?
I can handle love,
But not when it's loving you.

Slipping into a coma?
Things are getting dark.
Where there was a fire
Is only now a spark.
Girl, I need your lovin'
Heal me with a touch.
Shock me back to livin'
With that love I need so much. Chorus 4x

Stay With Me‡

Lord, it's hard to carry this load,
Can't keep from stumbling as I go down this road.
Every dream is tattered and worn.
I'm lost in a storm,
    Just need to belong.
Please stay with me as I go.

Dazed, confused, life seems so vague.
Tell me it's meaning, I'm so far astray.
My heart knows that answer, it just doesn't care.
With all my affairs
    There's nobody there.
Please stay with me as I go.

These same ol' blues still bring me down.
Whatever you do, don't wake me.
I'm shattered please don't break me.
Just ease me gently to the ground.

[Repeat 1st verse to end]

Take Me Home‡

Dog tired, far from my bed.
Should be under covers,
But here I am instead.
Last train to nowhere,
Won't somebody take me home.

Too many cars, so many rails.
I've been prone to wander
Since I got out of jail.
Last train to nowhere,
Won't somebody take me home.

Chorus I:
Miles and miles of scenery.
Doesn't do a damn thing for me.
Four walls would just do me fine.
If I could just find one place to call mine.

Brown paper bags, stale chips, warm beer
Stuck in Life's caboose
I need to get on out of here.
Last train to nowhere,
Won't somebody take me home.

(Chorus II:
Miles and mile of scenery
Is like pound for pound of misery.
Four walls would just do me fine,
If I could just find one place to call mine.

[Repeat 1st verse to end]

Walkin' Shoes‡

I've lived hard and I've lived alone,
Called it lucky when got tossed a bone.
When there's no way I can pay my dues,
I put on my walkin' shoes.

I'd squeeze a dime without any shame.
Scratchin', scrapping, -- my claim to fame.
Stay long enough to stir up bad news,
Then I put on my walkin' shoes.

Bridge:
Sometimes I walk the street 'till dawn,
Pretending I'm on my way back home.
But, there's nobody there
Who remotely looks like you.
Guess I'll keep on my walkin' shoes.

Bones tired, aching and cold.
Sometimes I feel there's a hole in my soul.
Can't keep still, got to get with the groove,
So, I put on my walkin' shoes.

When your down and feeling depressed,
Rise on up child, get out of that mess.
Put on some reds, take off the blues,
And put on,
I said put on,
Yeah, put on you walkin' shoes.

What say you and I go for a stroll.

Best Part of Me‡

Do what you want, say what you will.
    Come what may child, I'll love you still.
You found the key to my heart,
    Now you're the best part of me.

Our rising sun won't alway shine.
    Clouds may come girl, you'll still be mine.
As long as there's a ray of love,
    You're all I ever need.

I won't try to gloss things over,
    With promises I just can't keep.
As long as we can talk things over,
    Just you and me.

Do what you want, say what you will.
    Come what may child, I'll love you still.
You found the key to my heart,
    Now you're the best part
        You're the best part
            You're the best part of me.

For a Little While

Stay with me,
Hold me in you arms,
Neath your lovin' smile
For a little while.

Hold me near,
Sing you lullaby,
See me as your child
For a little while.

Chorus:
A healing touch away.
I need your touch today,
Hold me like a baby in you arms,
Like a baby in you arms.

Talk to me,
Soothe my aching heart,
In your simple style
For a little while.

Dry my tears,
Kiss away the dark.
Oh, how I need you now,
For a little while.

(Chorus, 1st verse and chorus.)

Silk and Lace

Yes it's true, you is my one desire,
Only you can set my soul on fire.
Day's dawning, I'm yawning
Lord it's good to see your face.
I'm your burlap, you're my silk and lace.

Mornin' cookin' sets my mouth to water.
So good lookin' there ought to be a law.
Eggs frying, I'm trying,
Come on let me sneak a taste.
I'm your burlap, you're my silk and lace.

Bridge:
Some can't believe that we're a pair.
Cause you can't take me anywhere. (Who cares?)

Loving you is only gettin' better.
Touch my heart, I'm floating like a feather.
Sounds crazy, but baby,
Your smile lights up the place
I'm your burlap, you're my silk and lace.

Love Sick Blues‡

I got the lonely, one and only,
    Can't sleep at all love sick blues.
I got the yearnin', the burnin',
    Hard to ignore love sick blues.

    Chorus I:
    Because you're givin' me doubts.
    I can't figure out if you love me like you say you do.
    I got the insecure, not so sure, need a cure,
    Love sick blues.

I got the carin', the swearin'
    Pacin' the floor love sick blues.
I got the bruisin', confusin',
    Don't know the score love sick blues.

    (Chorus I:)

I got the lonely, one and only,
    Can't sleep at all love sick blues.
I got the bruisin', confusin',
    Don't know the score love sick blues.

    Chorus II:
    Because you're givin' me doubts.
    I can't figure out if you love me like you say you do.
    I got the insecure, not so sure,
    Can't figure it honey,
        You take me high, then leave me dry,
                Why, why, why, why?
        I got the insecure, not so sure, need a cure
        Love sick blues.

Ding-Dong School of the Hard-Luck Blues‡

(Written with Keith Gonzales)

Lost forever, Lord, she's gone,
There's no denying, she ain't ever comin' home.
I didn't know it, but she sent me to school.
Ding-dong school of the hard-luck blues.

Won't answer my letters, not even one call.
Alone in my darkness with no light at all.
It's there in my papers, "Enroll this fool."
Ding-dong School of the Hard-Luck Blues.

Bridge I:
And every tomorrow,
With Professor Sorrow,
We'll be toastin' that last refrain.
Tellin' ol' stories
Of love and glory,
But that's all that will remain.

I'm lost forever, cause she's gone.
There's no denying, she ain't ever comin' home.
I didn't know it, but she sent me to school.
Ding-dong School of the Hard-Luck Blues.

Bridge II:
With every lesson,
There's manic depression,
From just knowin' I'll make the grade.
Some call me a failure.
But let tell ya,
They're gonna give this ol' boy an "A."

Repeat above verse.

Let Me See You Home

Hey, sweet lady, are you here all alone?
Is there someone who could take you home?
Yeah, I know it's not my place,
I just wanna see you safely home.

To tell the truth girl, it's kind-a late.
You know it's funny, some might call it fate.
How it's going on three
And just you and me,
Girl, let me take you home.

Bridge:
If you prefer to call someone,
I'll wait with you.
Or if you prefer, I'll just leave you alone.
But if something, God forbid
Should happen to you girl.
Your hurt would be my own.

So, sweet lady, since you're here alone,
I'm that someone willing to take you home.
Yeah, I know it's not my place.
I just wanna see you home,
You know I do.
I know my place, it's here by your side,
Every step along the road,
I just wanna make sure pretty lady,
That you get safely home.

Living With the Truth -- You're Gone

As I look out my window
The sun is falling.
The wind come in whispers
As the night fills the sky.
And on the horizon
I now see tomorrow,
Cause yesterday's memories
Are still in my eyes.

The streets are all crowded
With faces so empty.
And hearts are as hard
As this concrete below.
I go through the motions.
Live like a zombie,
Cause love caused a fire
And left a deep hole.

Chorus:
Oh, what you've done to me.
Oh, no, no, no, no, no.
I should just let it be,
But it's so hard gettin' over you,
Livin' with the truth -- you're gone.

I sit in my corner,
Play with my coffee.
Hands start to tremble
As tears fill my eyes.
From every direction,
My world comes to bleed me.
I stay to the shadows
Just to survive.

Chorus:

Bridge:
I stumble with every step I take.
With every move, I hesitate.
Cause ever time I hear your name,
I need your love again.

Interlude to chorus and 1 st verse.

Blues of a Soldier

I'm on the hard side of sorrow,
The closest thing to hell.
There's little chance of healing me,
I'm so deep inside the well.

Chorus I:
Lord, I've done things
And there's no place left to hide
Oh, these blues of a soldier,
Oh, these blues of a soldier,
Oh, these blues of a soldier
Will stay with me till the day I die.

The tears that fall from Heaven,
I just can't wash away.
The wailing cries that fill the skies,
Drown out each prayer I pray.

Chorus II:
Lord, I've heard things
That could make grown men cry
Oh, these blues of a soldier,
Oh, these blues of a soldier,
Oh, these blues of a soldier
Will stay with me till the day I die.

The memories of my brothers,
Who in this darkness fell.
The empty space that was their place,
(We know it all too well)
Their stories ours to tell.

Chorus III:
Lord, I seen things
　　Forever burning in my eyes
Oh, these blues of a soldier,
Oh, these blues of a soldier,
Oh, these blues of a soldier
　　Will stay with me till the day I die.

Rain Man

Clouds in the sky roll to my location,
Summoned by the Blues, the heart of my vocation.
Some call it magic, others think it strange,
To walk out in the sun, neath a cloud of pourin' rain.

Chorus, 2x:
Rain man, Rain man,
Sitting in the mud,
If Blues is like water
Then I'm drownin' in a flood.

Storms always find me, tears never dry,
Memories how they linger in the shadows of my eyes.
Some offer pity, others can't explain,
Me cryin' in the sun and laughin' in the rain.

Chorus 2x:

Bridge:
What I'd give to feel dry land
Gathered neath my feet
And not one drop of water,
But these blues won't let me be.

Chorus 2x:

Water keeps on risin', levy's bout to fail,
Blues hittin' hard, like a hammer to a nail.
Some say it's tragic, others what a shame
Even undercover, he's standin' in the rain.

(Chorus, 2x, retard ending.)

Come on In

Come on in, sit a spell
Some y'all tired, don't look too well.

Got a thorn stuck in da paw?
You make a man rich, while still livin' poor.

Chorus:
Hell, let's chew the fat,
Let's clean the slate,
Leave your money at the gate.
Just let's it go,
Untie your shoes.
Come on in, let's talk some blues.

Gnaw some grub, sip some beer,
Chase your pain up on out of here.

Stomp your foot, raise a glass
Just make sure you pay in cash.

Chorus

You might feel good,
You might feel sad,
But after a while,
I said, after a while,
You're gonna feel so glad.

Is It True What They Say About You?

I've only known you for what seems a short time.
But pretty lady, I wanna make you mine.
But before you answer and say, "I do,"

Chorus I:
Is it true what they say about you?
Is it true what they say about you?

New every rumor is a bold-face lie,
And I'm aware of those who signify.
For clarity I need you point of view.

Chorus I:

Bridge:
I understand your mad reaction,
But if you were me,
You'd want some satisfaction.

Girl, I still love you, I must confess,
But now then to second guess.
So, t his is the last time, just be true.

Chorus II:
Is it true what they say about you?
Is it true what they say?
True what they say?
Is it true what they say about
You know who?

Song Lyrics From 2011 to 2020..

What Could Have Been Your Life

Three in the morning, gin in a glass.
A curse for every year gone pass.
Time is like a stone,
And you're all alone
Wonderin' what could have been your life.

Peanuts on the bar trickle through your hands,
Like so many dreams, so many plans.
Never in the game,
But always finding blame.
Imagine what could have been your life.

Bridge:
With every move
There's a bad reaction.
For every dream
Someone else's came true.
Guess it's true
Can't get no satisfaction.
Sittin' there doin' what you do.

Three in the morning, gin in a glass.
Face in a mirror, lost in the past.
In yesterday's song
No one can belong,
Still, you wonder what could have been your life.

Was This Meeting by Design?

There's a madman in the corner
With drool down to his knees.
You give him your last dollar,
Now he just won't let you leave.

Yeah, the presence of his spirit
Awakens in your mind,
And there's that eerie feeling.
Was this meeting by design?

He mumbles out a thank you
As he fumbles with his change.
Adding, "Mom and Dad are worried."
And refers to them by name.

With both of them in Heaven,
There's a tingle in you spine.
You tussle with the question,
Was this meeting by design?

You gather up your reason
And try to make some sense.
For you are not in Kansas
Yet, you feel you need defense.

After all, he's just a madman
Sent here to do his time,
No way by a hair's breath
Was this meeting by design

For you have never been here.
And this madman you would know.
For you would see him coming,
Like a black dog in the snow.

Still he's giving you a message
For you to stay behind the line.
A madman or an angel,
Was this meeting by design? (Repeat and fade)

It Ain't Over

One more drink to end the night,
    One last cotton bail to tow.
Liberation is our right,
    We are free or so I'm told.
People moving 'long a trail,
    Leaving all behind but chance,
Just tell Massa, I took the rail,
    No more bailing, song, or dance.

    But it ain't over,
    Read a sign.
    They changed the music,
    But boy you're still mine.

In the north I labored hard,
    Took a wife and raised a child,
Drifting job from job to job,
    Felt the stress when things got wild.
I was told, you're free to dream,
    Just make sure you keep it real.
There's a line to everything,
    Know your place, we got a deal.

    For it ain't over,
    Flashed a sign.
    They changed the music,
    And boy you're still mine.

Bridge:
People on a holiday thinking they be free.
Shackled to a TV screen, telling them who to be.
Nation in a holding cell, sentenced by the few.
Listen to the cattle call, tell me it ain't you.

For it ain't over,
Just read the signs.
They changed the music
To control your mind.

There's a universal law,
There's a common bond we share.
Now some rich enslave the poor,
We should holler, we should care.
Come to understand the game,
Come to see who's playing who.
Learn the truth and go insane,
It's the least that you can do.

For it ain't over,
'Till we change the signs.
And rewrite the music
To free our minds.
(Repeat chorus and fade with 'free our mind")

Mary in the Garden

Mary in the garden,
Tending to her dreams
Neath the gray of city ruins
On a lonely patch of green.
Mary in the garden,
Flowers grace her hands.
No one knows her longings.
No, no one gives a damn.

Chorus I:
Each seed is her tomorrow
As rain falls night and day.
She reaches pass her sorrow
And wipes the tears away.

Mary in the garden,
Her soldier in his tomb.
She spies him by the rosebuds,
Walking with his wounds.
Mary in the garden,
Cries to the soul she sees.
Reveals a heart in mourning;
Full of wants, full of needs.

Chorus II:
Each seed is her for tomorrow,
Sprouting dreams of yesterday.
With no more love to borrow,
She begs him please, please stay.

Mary in the garden
Wrestling with her dreams
Neath the gray of city ruins
On a lonely patch of green.

Mary in the garden. (Repeat 3x and close.)

Take My Burden Down

Take my burden down,
I could use the rest.
Been travelin' so long
With this pound of flesh

Chorus I:
Lift this weight from me
Help me up on my feet
Take my burden down

You called me your friend,
Said you'd carry my load.
Well I'm calling in favors,
Just letting you know

Chorus I:

Bridge:
Been hounded by troubles unexpected,
Pursuing each path that I take
There are people out there undetected
Who just want to see me break

I've been there for you,
We've been here before.
Just a moment of peace,
Is all I'm asking for

Chorus I:

Chorus II
Lift this weight from me
Help me, won't you please
Take my
Take my   Take my burden down

Epilogue

I started playing guitar around 1964 – 65. It was an old Stella guitar my father had purchased in the 50s from a pawn shop on 145 Street between Broadway and Amsterdam Avenue. I remember him taking me up there with him. He might've been interested in learning to play music as he loved to listen to his jazz records. However, he never found the time, and the guitar found a nesting place under the basement stairs of our house in the Bronx once we joined the exodus out of Harlem, New York.

After listening to Bob Dylan, the Beatles, and other musical acts, some of my childhood friends were drawn to the medium. And so I found a passion I would never regret.

Over the years I was only able to publish two solo CDs.

†Crossroad (In the Rough) - CD

When You Play With Fire
One Can Never Tell
Workin' to Be Poor
Crossroad
Neath the City Lights
Stand Up, Stand Down
Then I See You
Your Eyes
Genocide
Love Is
Ain't No Blues
Amen (Instrumental with Donn Lowe)

‡The Best Part of Me - CD

Startin' All Over Again

Pain to Kill

Love Sick Blues

Drinkin' the Blues

The Best Part of Me

Help Me Out

Take Me Home

The Way of Things

Ding Dong School of the Hard Luck Blues

Stay With Me

Walkin' Shoes

Some songs can be heard in a video format on our Youtube channel (Amura Unlimited), along with some of my other ideas. Please take some time to listen.

Amurá Oñaā is an artist who dabbles in words, sculpts in wood and stone, dances with colors and paint brushes, and muses in lyrics and melodies, as well as a designer of tabletop games. Not much to tell because there's so much left to be discovered. Always finding ways to create "something." I enjoy introducing thought to the physical world and experiencing the response given. I'm just one aspect of life filling a niche. I hope you enjoy a part of my journey through the lyrics in the songs that I have written. It's hard not to hear the music, it's always playing along with the rhythms of the day. The universe if constantly broadcasting a vibratory tone called life.

Made in the USA
Middletown, DE
03 November 2023